I0048678

FROM AN INTERNATIONAL STUDENT

TO OWNING 30 PROPERTIES IN AUSTRALIA

A STEP-BY-STEP GUIDE TO

BUILDING YOUR PASSIVE INCOME

By Bharat Patel

De Fu Publishing

Website: www.defupublishing.com

E-mail: info@defupublishing.com

From an International Student

to Owning 30 Properties in Australia

A Step-by-Step Guide to Building Your Passive Income

Copyright©2025 Bharat Patel

Paperback ISBN: 978-1-922680-83-9

Ebook ISBN: 978-1-922680-84-6

Published by De Fu Publishing

1st edition, 2025

About the Author

Bharat Patel is the founder and director of Cashflow Properties, a company dedicated to helping people achieve financial freedom through property investment. Arriving in Australia from India in 2004 as an international student, he started with nothing. And today, with hard work and smart choices, he has built a property empire for himself.

In the beginning, like everyone else, real estate was clueless to him. After realising he wanted to retire by the age 40, Bharat dived into property investment. He learned step by step by surrounding himself with the right supportive team, planning carefully, and growing his property portfolio to 32 properties (by the end of 2024.)

Bharat's passion also lies in sharing his knowledge to help others achieve similar success. He founded Cashflow Properties in 2021 to make property investment accessible for everyone. Featured in the Daily Telegraph, Realestate. com.au, and the Courier Mail, Bharat's expertise and inspiring story have empowered countless Australians to take control of their financial future.

Bharat's story is proof that financial freedom through property investment is attainable. In this book, he shares his journey, insights, and proven strategies to help you find your own path to financial independence.

Introduction

If you Google search my name, *Bharat Patel*, a few news articles will pop up, with headlines like 'A migrant couple shares their remarkable journey of building a property empire worth $11 million' and '30+ properties in Australia... Here's how Bharat Patel did it.'

My wife and I maintain a portfolio of more than 30 residential properties and our investment journey started in 2008. We started our property investment with a household income of AUD38,000. Today, our portfolio is over $11 million and our rental income from all properties is about $600,000.

Well, what does all this mean to you?

Let me tell you, these big, nice numbers are the outcome of a 20-year journey in Australia. Just like every other international student, I came to Australia in 2004 with many dreams. I pursued my studies, did part-time jobs, graduated, joined the working world, got married, had our first child and bought my first home.

This is the usual narrative we hear from family and friends. Buying one home is deemed to be the pinnacle of achievement. Well, it could have been, back in earlier days.

But now times have changed. After buying my first home, I wanted to know more about real estate and thus my healthy hunger for property investment began. Becoming a real estate investor didn't happen overnight. I became a confident investor building 30 properties in my personal portfolio.

And you can do it too.

I've written this book, not just to tell my story but to educate and inspire anyone reading this book. You're probably at the early stages of settling in Australia, or you probably have bought your first home, or you are thinking of investment properties. No matter what stage you are at right now, with long-term vision and a proper strategy, you too can become an investor.

I'm living proof of how it can be done. This is not a rags-to-riches story that you might see in films. This is a real story of how hard work, determination and the right mindset can make financial freedom a reality.

Many books about real estate have been published. This book is unique because I'm going to tell you exactly how I started my real estate journey with real figures and data and how it was back in 2004 till today (2025). There are no gimmicks or fabricated stories here. Everything shared in this book has happened in my life.

This book is special because this is probably the first time an Indian migrant has written a book about real estate in Australia. You will resonate with the journey, struggles and the victory.

This book is to share my journey of how it happened and most importantly, why it is important for you to understand the real meaning of time and financial freedom. This book will let you unlearn and relearn how you can make real estate work for you. As I always joke with my family and friends and clients of Cashflow Properties (my company), "I don't like cash. I like cashflow."

A Major Milestone!

20 Properties and Counting!

How do you actually read this book?

This book is written for you to understand and break the old traditional rule: you can only retire at 65. You should not be aiming to retire at 65 with one property you bought 30 years ago. Instead, you should have a goal to retire at any age you want with a solid passive income.

This book is written for you to sit down and reconsider your life choices.

Do you want to keep working till 65?

Again, ask yourself, 'Why did you make the big move to Australia?'

You could be someone who moved here recently, or 5 years ago, or maybe 2 decades ago. If you were back in your home country, what would you have done with your life?

You moved to Australia for a better life. If you end up living the same life that you would be back in your home country, then did you make the right choice?

This book is my journey from the beginning days as an international student in Sydney in 2004 to the stage where I've built my passive income through property investment and technically have retired at the age of 40.

If you want to jump straight into property investment strategies, then you may skip to Chapter 4 where I talk about investing in my first property and how I gradually levelled up.

At the end of chapter 7, I've summarised the checklist to buy a property if you're planning to do so with a detailed checklist of figures that you need to know.

If you want to know my journey as an international student moving to Sydney in 2004, and starting life as a young boy completely clueless in a new country, then continue reading.

Table of Contents

i) About the Author 1

ii) Introduction 3

iii) How do you actually read this book? 7

Chapter 1:

Life in Australia as an International Student 1

Chapter 2:

Path to Making Australia my Home 19

Chapter 3:

Rent Money is Dead Money Back Then 37

Chapter 4: Building a Property Portfolio

on $38,000 Annual Income (Property 1- 15) 53

Chapter 5: Don't Listen to People

Who Aren't Savvy Investors! (Property 16-30) ... 109

Chapter 6: Think Big. Start Small 145

Chapter 7: Conclusion 159

A checklist to buy your investment property 168

Chapter 1

Life in Australia as an International student

The new beginning

15th February 2004.

The 18-hour flight from India to Sydney was a whirlwind of excitement and anxiety. My mind was bombarded with emotions, flashing vivid images of my parents and my fiancée, who I was leaving behind.

I could almost see my mother's tearful eyes and feel my father's strong, yet hesitant, embrace. My fiancée's face, filled with a mix of pride and sadness, haunted my thoughts, making my heart ache with the weight of separation. As the plane soared through the sky, I couldn't help but replay our goodbyes, the bittersweet farewell marking the beginning of a new, uncertain journey.

This was the beginning of my journey as a 22-year-old international student at the University of Technology, Sydney, to pursue my dreams of doing a Master's Degree in Computer Networking.

As I carried my luggage from the conveyor belt at Sydney International Airport, I was relieved that I landed safely. Coming from Ahmedabad, the Sydney surroundings were a stark contrast to what I was used to, and it hit me that my adventure had truly begun.

I walked out of the airport.

The unforgiving heat welcomed me with open arms of humidity.

My friend, with whom I did a Bachelor's degree programme in India, came to the airport to pick me up. He was the one who encouraged me to apply for a student visa in Australia. We both applied at the same time, and he arrived in Sydney one week before me.

He was staying in a suburb near the airport. He brought me to his place first. I spent half a day there. After that, he dropped me off at Strathfield (Sydney) where my apartment was. He couldn't accommodate me at his place since the apartment was occupied by a few friends. I was still feeling blank and clueless and just went with the flow. Too many thoughts were in my mind, and I just followed him to Strathfield.

Every minute, I was trying to consume what was happening around me. I had no idea about how renting worked in Australia, though I was fortunate that I had a place to stay in Strathfield in a 3-bedroom apartment shared by 8 other people.

Other uncertainties and worries overwhelmed me every day:

Can I even survive for a week?

I am a vegetarian. Where do I buy food?

Where was the bus stop?

During the first week, an overwhelming sense of anxiety constricted my chest, causing me to question my life choices:

Why did I even decide to come to Australia?

This was 2004. There was no smartphone, no internet, no WhatsApp, no Instagram, no Facebook, no easy mode of communication in 2004.

The only way to contact the family was through a Telstra booth phone call. I bought a Telstra card given by the company, and then I inserted the card in the phone and called my family members. It was way too expensive.

For a $20 card, I could barely speak for 10 to 15 minutes. And even in those 10 minutes, I didn't want to say much, either. I didn't want to discuss my problems. I just wanted to say "All is fine here, take care of yourself, call you next week."

That's how I started my life in Australia in the first week.

My first week
at the University of Technology in Sydney

I was 22. A young adult.

But in a new country, I was figuring out everything like a newborn baby.

I had to attend University the second day I landed in Australia. As I was already one week late for the course, one of the seniors in the programme gave me a quick 10-min orientation: inside and outside the university.

After that, they said "OK, figure out where your classrooms are and who your teachers are."

My friend who came to pick me up from the airport was on the same course. That gave me some confidence, hope and companionship. We relied on each other to find the information so we could help each other out.

The education system here was entirely different. In India, you always knew what to expect with subjects, books, and everything else. Even if you knew the course content here, it was way more detailed, and the teaching method was completely different. When I first started, I couldn't even figure out the timetable.

I chose my subjects, they gave me a timetable, and then there was a code number for the classroom. But before that, I had to figure out where the building was!

At UTS, we had three campuses really close to each other.

Forget about the course. I didn't understand:

how to get there,

how to find the building,

how to enter it,

how to go to classrooms, and

how to use my time,

The moment I was in the classroom, the teachers were expecting me to ask questions and start discussing the assignment and topic.

And at it took me at least for a month, to get into the routine of how university functioned here in Sydney. Gradually, I learnt the tricks to get things done fast and learnt the 'shortcuts'. Getting a book for an assignment in the library was always a challenge.

Why? Because there were only 2 or 3 copies.

Initially, I thought, "Oh that's fine; I have loads of time to get the book."

By the time I went to the library, the copies were gone. That was when I realised, I need to be fast. And then seniors taught me that if I was going to do that subject in advance, I needed to reserve the copy first.

I still remember a few nights when we preferred to

sleep in the library instead of going home – the place was just better than where I was living. It was really secure too, as no one from outside could get in. They had tea, coffee, milk, and all the usual stuff you needed.

After about a month and a half, I finally got the hang of things and made myself comfortable too.

Aussie Adventures!

Mr. Patel's First Time in the Stunning Blue Mountains!

New Friendships

Even building friendships was tough initially. To be honest, my Indian accent was tough for some people to understand. My first language was not English. I studied English medium back in India only when I did my Bachelor's degree.

Equally, it was hard for me to understand the Australian accent.

I had one American friend then. I couldn't really understand his accent. But he was very passionate and kind. He helped me to understand the culture as well. We also had a buddy system where seniors guided me in university.

Within the first 2 or 3 months, I became more confident. After that, I made many friends from India, China, Canada, Nepal and from other countries and also built a great rapport with the university professor and lecturers.

In terms of the cultural and lifestyle differences between India and Australia, the biggest cultural difference was the laid-back and casual attitude of the people here.

Part-time job and settling in

University studies, assignments, projects: I was pretty much occupied. It was a 2-year master's course. Every 6 months, I had to complete 3 to 4 modules. Despite a heavy academic schedule, part-time work was something that was on my mind because I wanted to self-sustain myself.

I had the chance to work for 20 hours a week as an international student. My first part-time job was at a car wash centre on the weekend. I was introduced to this job assignment by my friend. The car wash centre was located in the northern beaches of Sydney where rich people lived. They used to bring their expensive cars to this particular car wash centre.

Work usually started at 7am and if it was a sunny day, there would be hundreds of cars coming in. Work ended at 5pm and we didn't really get a break in between. It was just a constant 8 to 9 hours of work because I wanted to finish the 20 hours in 2 days.

That was the best time slot for me and I didn't want to travel back and forth between Strathfield and North Sydney.

Physically and mentally, it was draining, but that was

the best solution then.

While working at the car wash centre, I was already thinking of the next thing to do. I told myself, "If I can find something nearby in Strathfield that will be good."

I got a job at the fruit shop in Flemington during the weekdays. That was the next thing I did. The timing was very awkward. Reporting time was at 2.30am.

Yes, 2.30 in the morning!

Getting up at 2 am became the normal routine. No public transport at 2.30 am right! It was a 30-min walk from Strathfield to Flemington. A friend who also worked there accompanied me. That was my second job.

I continued my work at the fruit shop during my university days. Despite the awkward work reporting time, I liked this job. Because it was in the morning there was no traffic, so I was done with work by 8 am.

Once back home, I could solely focus on my university assignment. During the weekend, I had more time to myself too. Each dollar earned was giving me so much joy and confidence.

I was frugal with my money, cooking meals at home, using public transport and avoiding unnecessary expenses. Every penny saved was crucial for my future.

At the age of 22, my motivation was fuelled by a

desire to gain independence and build a life for myself here in Australia. This was more than just a journey of education; it was a journey of personal growth, resilience, and the relentless pursuit of my dreams.

Even meal preparation: I kept it simple. It was a challenge back then in 2004 to find Asian marts everywhere. Unlike the prevalence of Asian food everywhere now, I relied on a few items like bread, butter and noodles. Noodles were the easiest of course.

Two minutes.

Don't need to prepare too much for it. I got a few packets from Woollies and that was the food done.

As days passed by, I navigated my way to finding cheaper groceries and learnt cooking. My housemate taught me how to cook and also helped us with sharing their knowledge of how to get basic amenities, necessities and other stuff.

Spending every dollar like the last dollar

I was blessed to have no intense pressures from parents back home. The only question was: *Was I fine? How was I settling down? Was I comfortable with accommodation and finding new friends?*

They didn't demand anything from me, even though I took out an education loan for my studies. And my only goal was to study well, do well and not give any problems from my side to them.

Fees were the number one concern for international students: AUD $38,000 for a two-year Masters course. And this was an exorbitant amount in 2004. Now in 2024, I know a few students who are now paying $60,000 to $80,000, which is a lot of money for anyone.

I did not have any scholarships when I was studying. I took an education loan from the bank. The first semester fees were paid by the bank. My parents gave me about $5,000 for other expenses and I kept that as an emergency fund.

My greatest pressure wasn't academic; it was the burden of paying off my education loan. My thoughts constantly revolved around finding ways to earn money within the 20-hour work limit allowed for international students in Australia. It wasn't just the tuition fees I had to cover; there were also expenses for accommodation, daily living costs, and travel, which were all quite high.

I had to think 5 times before spending every single dollar.

Sometimes, when I felt hungry, I would be tempted to buy something to eat. But then I would remind myself that in just 30 minutes, I could be home and cook some noodles.

"Let me go home," I would tell myself.

"Let me cook my noodles, so I don't have to spend 10 dollars."

Snowy Escapades!

Unforgettable Fun in the Snowy Mountains!

18 months passed by like a breeze (and turbulence)

My strong focus was on my academic journey. I came here as a student and I wanted to fulfil that role to my fullest potential.

I knew a few friends whose mindset completely changed after arriving in Australia. For various reasons, they shifted to focus on earning money instead of focusing on their studies. I wasn't distracted by all that.

I was trying to settle myself down into the Australian way of life, understanding the culture, trying to focus on my communication and improving my skills so that at least I could go and give my resume to someone and start finding a job.

This was how my mind compartmentalises challenges and reaches deadlines:

Identify the problem - narrow down the problem - have a deadline - work out a solution from the bottom all the way up. For example, if I had an assignment with a two-week deadline, I would try to finish it a week early. That way, if I needed to make revisions, got new ideas, or faced any emergencies, I wouldn't have any stress. This approach helped me adjust to life in Australia.

In Australia, freedom of speech is highly valued.

People are more chilled and relaxed. Understanding cultural differences was also a major part of the first year in Australia. When I came here, initially I was greeting "Hi sir, Hi madam."

These greetings were common in India, but it was not the way here in Australia. I had to unlearn those practices and relearn new ways. Here, when you go to the shop, you have to casually ask "Hey, how's your day been?"

Learning new habits and practices were part of my personal growth. My body language changed too. I became confident communicating with everyone in Australia.

18 months passed by like a breeze, but with many strong winds I should say.

There were lots of initial challenges, lessons, joy and friendships.

It seemed like everything was going fine.

And then one day, a storm hit me.

I was told that my father suffered from a cardiac arrest in October 2006.

I could only go back to India in December 2006.

Chapter 2

The Path to
Making Australia my Home

I was about to graduate in 6 months.

I was creating a life for myself in Australia.

Now, when I heard about my father - I was shattered.

Will I continue staying in Australia? Do I go back home for good? Do I take a short break? What should I do?

But no matter what, life doesn't really prepare you for everything. My mind was numbed with thoughts and guilt as a son. I was emotionally down for more than a month.

For every drawback, there would be a blessing. My blessing in this situation was my fiancée. She gave me loads of confidence that my dad was recovering well in hospital. They did the bypass surgery, and he was out of danger.

They did not inform me until he was out of hospital and back home.

They did so because they didn't want me to get worried. That was a huge burden off my shoulders. They knew that I couldn't have done much from Australia. More than me, both my fiancée and my mother handled the situation well.

Again, I owe it to my fiancée, who was extremely supportive as she took care of my parents. She tried her best to fulfil my role as a son so that they did not feel like they were missing me.

My father was recovering well. And he was alive. Thank God.

With the strong support provided by my fiancée, I didn't visit him at this junction. I wanted to finish my course and apply for Permanent Residency first. I met the immigration lawyers, and they informed me that I was in a strong position for PR.

Back to My Roots!

First Trip Home from Australia to India!

How I met my fiancée

She was 18 when I first met her. Some people might laugh and people could say, "Wow, that's brave enough to make those kinds of decisions early in life."

It was tough for both her and me.

No phone. No text message. No social media platform like now. We had Yahoo Mail messages though.

Back then, it was just that Telstra phone booth and the card. Though it was expensive, I tried to call her once a week or fortnightly. All we had was 10 minutes over the phone.

When I was in India to get married, everything was organised. I was there for 1.5 months. My family members did their part to arrange everything right from booking the hall to food.

When she came to Australia in 2006, I applied for a spouse visa and included her in my PR.

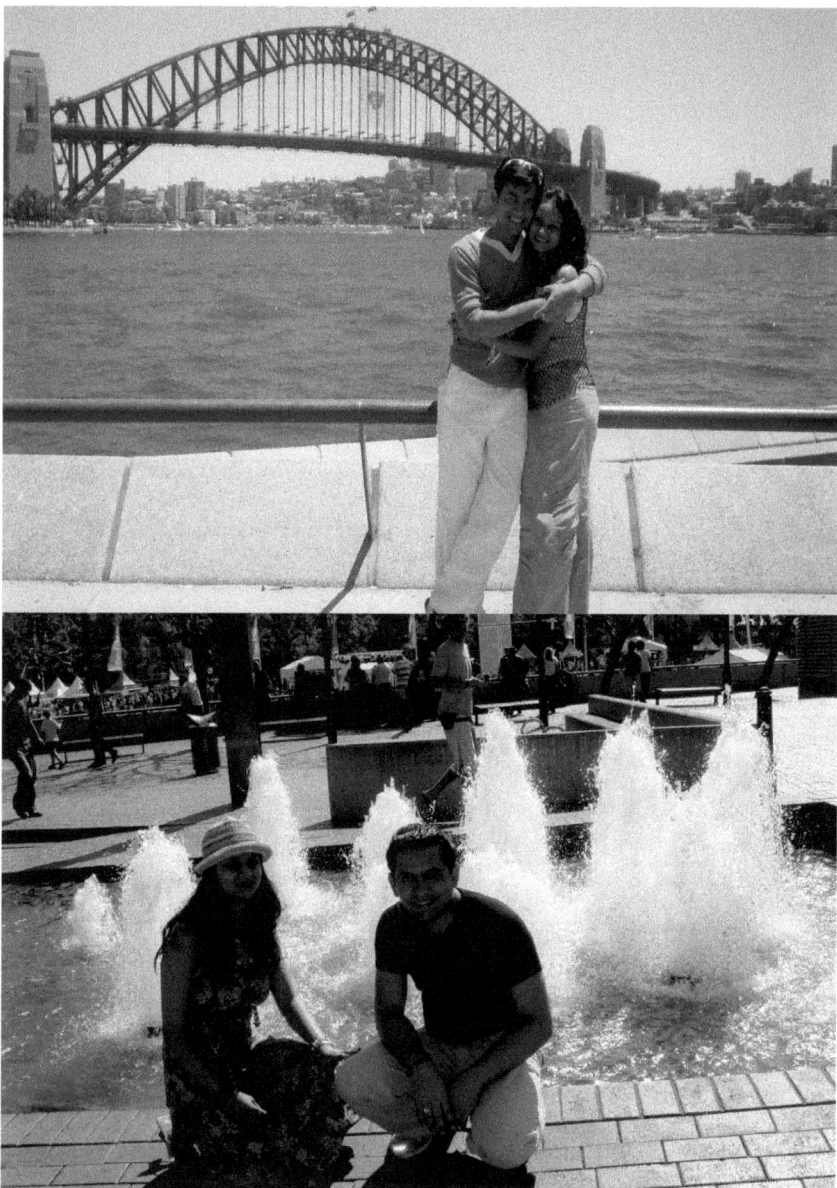

Reunited at Last!

Mr. & Mrs. Patel Together After Her First Aussie Visit!

Job search and upskilling

Once I graduated in 2006, I knew exactly my pathway.

In the IT field, back then, there were fewer people and fewer opportunities compared to now in Australia. I had just finished my course in computer networking, which was very lucrative at the time. It offered the potential for good jobs and good salaries. I was determined not to settle for labour jobs, fruit shop work, or car washes. I wanted to learn and grow in a corporate environment.

With this positive mindset, I began applying for jobs. It was initially challenging to understand the job requirements, but my education at the University of Technology Sydney had given me a solid foundation.

My first job in 2007 was as a first-level help desk support person. In this role, I picked up calls and helped customers resolve their IT-related problems like handling client inquiries, asked them to reset internet connections and unplug their internet cables. Though it was trivial, it made me understand how the corporate world worked. This experience was invaluable in launching my career in IT. This job was an entry level job, but my skill was a lot more than what was needed for that job.

I was constantly updating myself about the Australian

job market. Even with a full-time job, I applied to as many jobs as possible. I went for the interviews and spoke to many consultants. I did this frequently.

I would say preparation was a key to crack the market. I cracked it completely but I did not stop there. I upskilled myself, consistently and continuously.

Every single job I had, I learned a lot from it, and I was looking for the next big moment. My mindset was not to have one job and tell myself, "I'm done. This is enough for me."

Working in IT is all about honing your skills. If you're good at programming, that's awesome, but for me, it was all about networking. I kicked off my journey by getting the Cisco Certified Network Associate (CCNA) certification, which really opened doors for my first job.

On the job, I realised the importance of continuously getting more certifications to stay on top of my game. Each new certification not only widened my job prospects but also enhanced my skill set. In the IT world, having a solid mix of experience and recent certifications is key. This blend has been instrumental in my professional growth and career advancement.

My mindset was to secure a job, learn as much as I could while contributing my valuable inputs, and gain more skills and then move on to the next job. Again, repeat and rinse.

And it was not easy to change jobs and to grow.

Professionally, there was a lot of politics here as well. To overcome those kinds of challenges, as I said before, my mindset was clear.

I joined the company and worked diligently. I became an asset to the company and I learnt a lot of things from them, and then I looked for the next challenge.

That's exactly how I transitioned my career as an IT from one job to the next job. In terms of the company, I used to work in a company where there were 3 people, 5 people, 10 people, 500 people and even 1000 people.

In terms of accepting the culture's company size, I also gained a lot of experience dealing between the companies, between the different cultures, and between the teams.

From one level to the other level, I kept progressing: My last job in 2022 was as an IT manager before I started my own business.

Proud Moment!

Graduation Day at UTS—A Dream Achieved!!

Becoming Permanent Residents in Australia

While working, I was under a work visa. And in my permanent resident (PR) visa application, I added my wife's application too. She had to do her IELTS and everything. We were in a strong position to get our PR.

I successfully received my Australian Permanent Residency in 2008.

It took a little bit longer than expected. But that's how life is.

When she joined me in Australia, she went through the same struggle as me in getting to know the new environment, the culture, the language, the lifestyle.

Officially an Aussie!

Permanent Residency Secured!

Year 2007 to 2022:
Losing some, gaining some

15 years of growing personally and professionally. Now looking back, I thank myself, my wife, my parents and God.

The journey was full of ups and downs.

I married at an early age and by the time I had responsibilities and a wife, it was a life-changing experience.

But my friends were partying and having a different life. I had someone to look after, and she had to look after me.

My life certainly was different, my starting point was different, and my challenges were very different. By the time I finished my first job, I had to start finding the next accommodation as rental demand was crazy at that time.

I had to think about the next big thing in life, something that my friends didn't have to do.

First challenge: How do I help my wife to settle in Australia?

Second challenge: How can we together minimise our expenses, so that we can start thinking about the next moment?

I am always grateful that my wife and I have been on

the same frequency when it comes to money and finances till today.

We both had the same mindset: we were not after luxury items.

We thought about our necessities first. For example, if I could live in a small apartment, my wife would be equally comfortable, and she always supported me.

Grocery and food: We spent within budget. We planned ahead of any other new challenges for us. Because after spending that much money for my university course, my first reaction was: "how can I start saving some money so that I can pay down my debt back in India?"

And secondly, yes, I had some good friends. But I was in a different phase of life, facing different challenges. I tried to minimise contact with them and wanted to be in a tribe where I could meet like-minded individuals. The kind of friends who were couples and who were on a similar journey to me, so that at least I could meet them regularly with my wife.

I gradually changed my circle of friends.

I attended a few cultural events, beginning with worship at a temple. There, I met a variety of people who were on the same journey as me, many of whom also got married early. By participating in these events, I began to form connections with people who shared similar experiences and backgrounds, which helped me feel more connected and understood.

Find your right friends

In a migrant journey, especially people who are married, you may fall into the usual trap. You move to Australia, get a job, buy a house, get a car and you feel that that's the achievement level.

Ask yourself: Is that truly what you want?

But when you are doing it differently you have to take certain calculated risks and be ready to travel on an unconventional path. There is going to be 'noise' around you. It's all about accepting what you have instead of arguing what you don't have.

For example, when my friend asked me, "Hey, you want to come and join us for a party on Friday evening?"

I said, "No. I'm going to sit down at home in front of my computer to watch a movie with my wife."

In a way, I was also finding happiness at my own pace. We found our own joy in our comfort zone. When we did, we also saved some money as well. Instead of spending money on travelling and eating out, we tried to stay at home but also enjoyed life doing things together.

A Journey to Remember!

First Trip Home to India with My Wife!

Chapter 3

Rent Money was Dead Money Back Then

My wife and I were sharing a three-bedroom house in Strathfield with four friends who were living together. My wife and I occupied one bedroom, and the other four friends were in the remaining rooms.

Back then in 2008, the rent was $330 a week for the entire house. It was quite expensive. If you calculate it, $330 divided by six people meant everyone could afford the rent.

My wife was 20 and I was 23. I was appointed as an entry level worker in a telecommunication company and my pay was AUD 38,000 for the first 2 years. My wife wasn't working. We still managed with one income, and I was happily living my day-to-day life.

I started paying back my parents for the education loan that I took. They didn't ask me for money, but it was my duty to return the money. Any little amount would be good for them. I tried to save every single dollar and at the same time I had to save something in Australia

My goal was to save half of the $38,000 I received. My wife was not working. I was still continuing with the fruit market job even when I was working in that entry level IT role.

I worked during the weekend. Technically, I was working seven days a week. My plan was to get 50% savings from that corporate IT job. From that fruit market that I worked for 10 hours over the weekend gave me about $200. That totalled to about $1,000 a month. I tried to use that money to immediately send it back to my parents.

It was like an automated savings plan.

Buy necessities, not luxury

I liked the basic things that made me happier. Basically, my focus was to fulfil my necessities. Forget about luxury.

For example, if I had to choose an outfit between $20 and $60, and if both of them did the same job of making me look good, I would prefer the $20 shirt. My mindset was clear. Instead of thinking about the next luxury item, think about the basic necessities first.

I had a strong savings plan and I wanted to do some automation savings. My wife played a huge role in managing day-to-day expenses.

For example, most people hardly plan. They buy water bottles from the shop. And when they go out, they get a coffee and buy dinner outside. My wife and I take all the water bottles and food from home when we travel.

Actually, having a cup of coffee is fun for some. Let them have fun. But for me, if I can get something from my home and if I can save money, I'll stick to it. My wife was my motivator. She always reminded us to take water and food from home. Dinner time was mostly at home.

I hardly remember, right from 2006 up until 2010, visiting any restaurant in Australia. None at all.

Yes, I can't deny the temptations. I sometimes have a craving too,

"Let's go do this. Let's do that."

But my wife knew our plan, and she was with me with the same goals about what we wanted to do. We didn't lose much on enjoying life. We experienced the same happiness preparing meals at home.

And she was my best cheerleader and motivator, and I was also supporting her in her endeavours.

Use social media to your advantage

These days, the influence of social media is so strong - places, restaurants, new experiences, food. There is no harm done watching social media and scrolling through, as long as you know your goals. Because the moment you follow any restaurant, they will start feeding you their post every day. It's up to you to have some sort of control, some sort of discipline.

Watching social media ads doesn't mean you have to visit the restaurant. Have some discipline. Strike a balance between fun and overspending. Yes, it is possible to make money, spend money and save money as long as you have discipline.

I know people are not going to believe me and would say "Oh, currently we have too much inflation."

In reality, if you spend five dollars on a water bottle and six dollars on coffee and expensive stuff and expensive clothes, then you are making the (wrong) choices for yourself.

It is up to you to decide exactly what you need. You don't always have to visit restaurants. There is always going to be a noodle shop to get affordable food if you visit at 5 p.m. when they close their shops. They sell food for $8. You don't need to spend $22 for the same food in a restaurant or café.

You could buy tomatoes at $7 or $8 a kilo in the supermarket, but you can get a kilo of tomatoes at $4 if you know where to get them.

It's that little mindset shift. "I don't want to spend $7 per kilo of tomatoes, but I still want to eat tomatoes."

To begin your journey and to save some money, you have to put in the energy and time to source places where you can get things cheaper. Once you learn the art of doing it, you will not go back.

Even up to today, I buy my teenage son's jeans for $10 from one of the largest retailer's factory outlets.

Anything is available at a price that's more affordable; you just need to spend that extra time to find out. Spending time on social media to find expensive places or use the same platform to source the cheaper ones: **the choice is yours**.

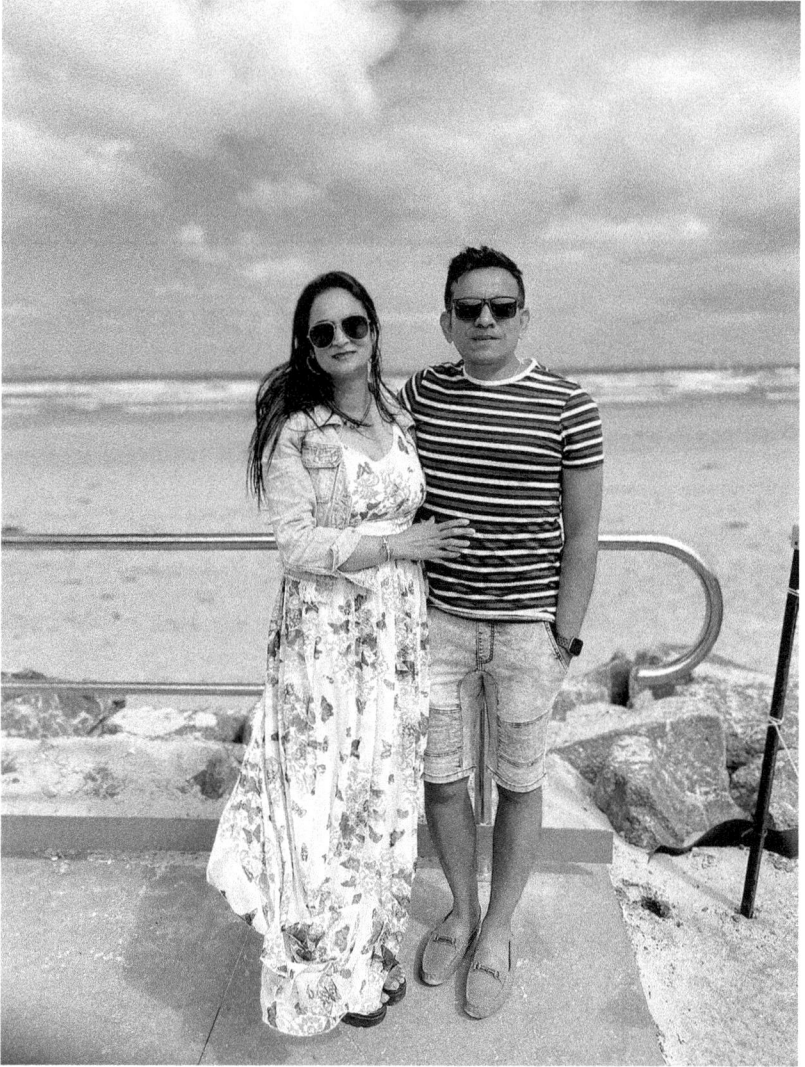

Another Huge Win!

Bharat & Vaishali Patel Celebrate 20 Properties
Bought on the Gold Coast!

Communicate your goals with your partner

None of our five fingers are quite the same. Likewise, your partner can never be quite the same as you. Even my wife was not on the same frequency as I was when I met her. But eventually it was all about open communication.

At the age of 22, when I met her, I said, "This is what I am doing in Australia. If you want to join me, initially, it will be tough. If we become successful, we don't need to work until we die."

There were a lot of questions. But then, ultimately, she was in finance. At least she has some sort of understanding of what I was explaining to her, she was able to judge my personality back then.

She understood my long-term plans. I reassured her that we could do it together if we aligned our plans together. That's how we agreed with each other, and we just started life based on both of our circumstances.

Communicate with your partner about your lifestyle and future goals as most people never communicate with each other. That's why misunderstandings occur. That becomes a barrier to your future goals.

I literally had a paper and pen, and we wrote down our goals together.

At 24.........

At 30....

At 40......

This isn't easy. It requires a lot of time, dedication, and energy. But if we can break a large, complex problem into smaller pieces and stick together, it's definitely possible to achieve our goals even today.

The way I see it, you need to treat your partner with respect, just as you expect them to respect you. Both partners need to sit down, understand each other, and come to a mutual commitment. It's not about one person working hard while the other doesn't; both partners need to put in the effort and work smart together.

In Australia, people work until 70, and they have very little money in their accounts or superannuation. They don't have any savings.

When I told my wife, "I don't want to live a life where I have to work until I die."

I want to work for 10 years. And then I just have to live my life in auto mode where everything will be automated. I don't have to worry about the economy, interest rates, inflation, earning money and savings as long as I can build the system.

I want to be my own bank. I was very confident that

I could do it.

Sydney Magic!

Mr. & Mrs. Patel Soaking up Views of Darling Harbour!

Time to move out to my own apartment

Eventually, I found something in Strathfield - a small one-bedroom studio that I secured for $220 a week. It was perfect for my wife and I to start our new life together.

But it was very tiny, almost nothing - a simple room with a small kitchen. Still, I thought, "At least let me start somewhere." If I hadn't decided to move out from my friends' place, I wouldn't have learned how to manage life in my own apartment. I was always in my comfort zone, and I wanted to leave it to see what life would be like on the other side. In 2007, my wife and I started renting the studio in Strathfield for $220 a week.

We moved from Strathfield to Homebush, then to Parramatta, and finally to Seven Hills. Since 2007, I kept trying to push further out because everything was getting more expensive, and rent kept increasing. Honestly, I had no clue what to do, but I learned along the way.

Rents increased again.

Then we moved out. The new landlord said they would give me only six months and then six months later they said, "Oh, we have to increase the rent."

Then we moved out again. Every time the rent increased I found another place for the same $220/week that I wanted to pay.

We started in Strathfield, which was 14 km away from the city, and over the next few years, we moved further away and ended up in Seven Hills, which was 35 km away from the city.

Frustration was the right word to describe this entire period.

My first son was born in 2008. We had to keep moving with our little one, and it was incredibly challenging.

As a father, I felt a deep urge to provide stability and security for my family. I wanted to give my wife, my child, and myself a place we could truly call home. This responsibility drove me to push beyond my comfort zone and find a way to secure a stable future for us. Every move was a step towards creating a better life for my family, and that motivation kept me going.

Back then, it was all about figuring out where I could rent, how to save enough to stay put so my wife and I wouldn't have to keep moving. Moving from one place to another gave me a lot of confidence and taught me to think outside the box. It made me realise that I could handle these challenges and eventually find a way to buy our own home.

That's when I realised I needed to educate myself

about buying a home in Australia. I knew I had to learn the steps and understand the process to secure a place of our own.

From 2007 to 2010, I moved several times. I didn't want to move out. I wanted to stay somewhere permanently. I bought my first home in Doonside in Western Sydney at an auction in 2010.

This was the start of my real estate journey.

Dream Big, Achieve Bigger!

Build the Future of Your Dreams!

Chapter 4

Building a Property Portfolio

on a $38000 annual Income

(Properties 1-15)

More than buying a home, getting out of the rent cycle was my first priority. We were mentally exhausted, moving from one rental accommodation to another for almost 3 years.

I remembered one of my university buddies informing me that he met a mortgage broker. He got his pre-approval and he asked me to join and do the same thing. I had no idea about how a pre-approval worked.

That term was totally new: What exactly was it?

I just met a broker and received a pre-approval of about $330,000 to $340,000 based on my $38,000 annual income. The interest rate was more than 7% back then in 2010. In 2008, the interest rate was skyrocketing during the Global Financial Crisis.

I had my pre-approval.

Next, the real problem: Where can I find a good property?

Having pre-approval didn't mean anything. It was just a paper document to indicate that I could buy a property.

How will I find the property which ticks the boxes for my needs?

How will I make sure the property will grow?

How will I make sure the property will not have a problem?

My mind was bombarded with more questions than

ever.

But I knew I really wanted to buy a home soon. I had the deposit. I was also working two jobs, 7 days a week. My broker was very supportive. He was from Malaysia and a migrant like me who had made Australia his home. He knew what I wanted.

He advised me, "Hey, this is Australia; you need to be aware of a few things. You need to make sure you understand the process before you sign any documents. You need to know exactly why you chose a property - check the amenities and location."

And that got me to list a few important factors, even though I was still clueless about what to look out for, or what to avoid. This was 2010 when Google Search was barely a thing. And back then, when you signed up with a real estate agent, they would text you the open homes on your mobile. They would give you the list of the properties.

Honestly, all this information was overwhelming. I was not researching the locations at all. For me, I was only looking at two things.

i) Number one, this property must be within my borrowing capacity.

ii) Number two, the mortgage repayments must be

the same as the rent that I was previously paying.

My borrowing capacity was about 340K.

This was a huge decision. As a couple, we had a conversation about our life goals. We were on the same page: we didn't want something shiny or a fancy property.

Most people invest their emotions in their home and think that would be their forever home. Our intention was to escape from the rent cycle. Every home buyer, especially a first-time investor or buyer goes through a similar emotional cycle: *Am I buying the right thing? Am I doing the right thing? Should I wait any longer? Should I ask someone?*

But what gave me confidence was the numbers: Instead of giving away rent, we were using the same amount for a mortgage. That made sense. We bought our first home that had a simple basic layout. Nothing luxurious - 3 bedrooms, 1 bathroom and a kitchen and that was it.

We moved into our home after my son's birthday. September 2010. And I bought my home (Property 1) at an auction. I attended the auction on my own. There were 50 people at the auction. I was almost paralysed with fear while I was going through the auction. I'd already missed out on so many properties prior to this one. I didn't want to let go of this opportunity.

Back in 2010, the government also gave a cashback offer of $14,000 for first time home buyers. If I had bought a new home, I would have received $21,000. So, for established homes, it was $14,000.

The property journey begins

Property 1

Year purchased: 2010

Purchase Price: $322,000, No stamp duty, $14,000 back from Government

Configuration: 3-1-1

Land Size: 700sqm

Location: Western Sydney

Capital Expenses to purchase property at 20 % Deposits	
Purchase Price	$322,000
Loan amount required	$257,600
Deposits at 20 %	$64,400
Stamp duty	$0
Legal Expenses	$700
Building and pest inspections reports	$400
Buffer	
Total	**$65,500**

Expenses	Weekly ($)	Monthly ($)	Annually ($)
Council rates	$23.08	$100.00	$1,200
Strata Fees	-	-	-
Water rates	$21.15	$91.67	$1,100
Building / Landlord insurance	$15.38	$66.67	$8,00
Management fees	-	-	-
Mortgage Repayments	$190.62	$826.00	$9,912
Estimated Totals	**$250.23**	**$1,084.33**	**$13,012.00**

Estimated Income			
Lower Rent	$340	$1473.33	$17,860
Higher Rent	$380	$1646.67	$19760.00

Estimated cash flow before any tax considerations			
Lower Rent	$89.77	$389.00	$4,668.00
Higher Rent	$129.77	$562.33	$6,748.00

An auction, like we all know, is usually like a boxing match.

At that moment, I had no idea what was happening. I calculated the deposit I had and the mortgage payments I had to make. When they announced $315k, I was literally shaking. I quickly listed down the numbers and asked myself if I could go higher, and yes, I got it at $322K.

This was the period when the market was bouncing back from a bad period of recession. The market was still 'gentle'. And I took advantage of that.

Back then, I didn't even know how to read the building and pest report. What was a building and pest report? When you sign the contract, you would ask for a building and pest inspection. The report would show findings of the condition and other defects in the house. Back then, I didn't even know how to comprehend the whole thing.

I accepted everything the agent gave me. I received the report and looked at the agent and told him, "I hope you gave me a good property."

I was glad that it had a huge land size. Not having to pay rent thereafter was the best feeling in the world. But this was a 30-year mortgage and I knew this was a long-term commitment. It felt surreal to own something. On the brighter side, I was paying nearly the same amount for my mortgage repayment as I had done in rent.

There was a backyard for my son to play. We could do the decor we liked: hang pictures, decorate as we liked. It was a massive achievement.

But the next thing that was running in my mind: What's next?

I was reading many articles and spent lots of time on understanding real estate and managing money. At that time, I came across the concept of granny flats. It was a new concept in 2011. The first thing I knew: I can build a flat in the backyard.

That was new to me and many Australians.

The council was happily giving approval to build and sub divide. As much as it helped individual investors, it helped the nation because new homes were built. And this meant accommodation needs were taken care of.

Was this a way to earn a second income? - I asked myself several times before making the move. Then I started learning everything about the process of building a granny flat. I applied for a builder's license from fair trading. In this way, I could get my own tradesman and save on the cost of building a granny flat.

My first granny flat: 3-bedroom flat at the backyard of my home.

It was a huge project. However, the tradesman community was well-connected. As I knew the tradie guy, he gave me contacts for everyone else: electrician, plumber and the whole team.

I was managing the project: "Ok you do the slab. The next one can do the frames. Another fellow does the roof..."

I did all the bits and pieces together while I was working full time as an IT manager.

First Big Investment!
How I Scored My First Aussie Property at Auction for $322K!

Building a Granny Flat

Property 2

Year Built: 2012 (Owner builder project)

Purchase Price: $65,000

Configuration: 3 -1-1

Land Size: 700 sqm

Location: Western Sydney, subdivided into granny flat - 3 beds

Construction Costs: $65,000

Capital Expenses to purchase property at 20 % Deposits	
Purchase Price	$65,000
Loan amount required	-
Deposits at 20 %	-
Stamp duty	-
Legal Expenses	-
Building and pest inspections reports	-
Buffer	-
Total	$65,000

Expenses	Weekly ($)	Monthly ($)	Annually ($)
Council rates	-	-	-
Strata Fees	-	-	-
Water rates	-	-	-
Building / Landlord insurance	$7.60	$32.92	$395.00
Management fees	$16.50	$71.50	$858.00
Mortgage Repayments	-	-	-
Estimated Totals	$24.10	$104.42	$1253.00

Estimated Income			
Lower Rent	$330	$1,430.00	$17,160.00
Higher Rent	$380	$1646.67	$19,760.00

Estimated cash flow before any tax considerations			
Lower Rent	$305.90	$1325.58	$15,907.00
Higher Rent	$355.90	$1542.25	$18,507.00

If I had gone with the builder, it could have cost me about $80,000. With a builder license of my own, I could cut costs.

Time taken to build: 6 months.

This was the combination of savings and equity from property 1. Back then, there was not too much of a construction crisis. House materials were relatively cheap too, unlike now in 2024, where a granny flat could cost about $180,000 (Sydney). And I completed my builder's license for about $1,000.

The next challenge was of course to get tenants. The property managers were charging a 6% management fee. I thought if someone was living in my backyard, let me manage it myself. Hence, I just advertised my granny flat on Gumtree. The new tenants signed the lease agreement within two weeks after the advertisement.

Rent for the granny flat: $280/week

The house I was living in had a mortgage of $1,600 a month. The rental income from my granny flat was covering more than half of my home mortgage. The plan was to pay down my home mortgage and thus my borrowing capacity could increase eventually.

This granny flat concept was a great deal back then. I was already thinking of boosting my borrowing capacity and the granny flat income was absolutely putting me on track. In this way, I was already planning for my next one.

That was how I understood the power of compounding growth, the power of and the knowledge of finance. I had my home and one rental property in my backyard.

When friends got to know about it, their reaction was mixed. Some people didn't like other people's success. Some people were envious.

Holding costs, expenses and managing tenants, "Wasn't this more hassle for you?" they asked.

Instead of congratulating me, they warned me, "be aware of the tenants."

These people never fail to inject fear.

They continued, "You never know who you are dealing with."

This was also why I always believed that the people you mix with break or make you.

Despite all this warnings of chaos, I had a very good friend who was genuinely happy for me. He was the real estate agent that I had built a rapport with. He was the one I bought my first property from. He had been cheering me on since day 1.

My backyard was massive. Now with a granny flat, at least, I didn't have to worry about maintaining the grass.

The 'grass' was actually giving me rental income. Who wouldn't want that?

Is there a term called property portfolio?

From 2012 to 2015, it was a learning period to understand how to build a property portfolio. The term property portfolio was not even coined back then. Having tasted success with property 1 and 2, I knew that this could be repeated.

The Excel Sheet was my best friend. Numbers mean everything. Zero emotions.

In terms of return on investment, this seemed like the right path. It was giving good cash flow on top of what I was earning. I also had tax depreciation from the granny flat (property 2)

My next question, of course, was: Can I borrow more? What will be my next borrowing capacity?

I was constantly meeting brokers to find out about my borrowing power and my next plan and the places to buy. From 2012 to 2015, I didn't have that much income. Thus, I had to wait 3 years to get more borrowing power.

Though 3 years was a long period, I read and analysed how to make my investment affordable in some way. I wanted to maintain the same lifestyle while investing and also receive more rental income.

Why more rental income? More rental income meant I could boost my overall income. In the eyes of the banks, any property that generates income, they love it. So, do what the bank loves.

And my biggest motivating factor, other than building a property portfolio, was

'Why was I doing this?'

Knowing your 'WHY'

As readers, you've followed my journey so far, and you should also have this question in your mind: Why?

Because the 'why' is important.

Back in my university days, remember I used to do jobs at the car washing centre? For every car I washed, my mind was bombarded with, "What do these people do differently to afford nice cars?"

Everyone has 24 hours a day. Do these people have 48 hours a day?

Why can these people easily afford everything, and why can't I afford everything?

Not in a jealous kind of way. But sincerely, I wanted to know how they were doing it. And during those days I was inspired to create my income stream.

Many South-East Asians and the community I grew up in had a different view of savings. But I was not a fan of savings. Because savings are not going to give you financial freedom.

Investment does.

Understanding compounding growth is crucial. Compounding growth is powerful. Surprisingly, I didn't have a typical Indian mentality. Indians believe in savings and not doing anything with it.

I didn't care about savings. I cared more about cash flow. That was the reason why I named my company 'Cashflow Properties' too.

I love cash flow. I hate cash (parked in a place where no growth is happening)

The idea is simple and logical. Let's say you have a million dollars. What do you do with the million dollars? One day, that amount will be gone if no other income is generated from it.

But, imagine that a million dollars is giving you $30k. Isn't that the best way to grow your money? You don't need to worry about savings being depleted because there is going to be a constant cash flow. You can live your life the way you want from the cash flow. This logical idea meant a lot from day one.

You may wonder about other asset classes. For me, I had no interest in other asset classes. These days, there are things like crypto and stuff. I always believed in property.

Historically, one asset class that stayed strong was property/real estate. No matter how the world is going, real estate will be the winner. That is the power of property investing.

I believe why people fall for other quick schemes is because real estate needs time. Other asset classes may give you overnight success.

You can't make money overnight from property, right!

I don't want to be rich overnight. I want to have a comfortable life after 10 years.

Hence, I chose property investment.

Accumulating Properties 3-6

Property 3

Year purchased: 2015

Purchase Price: $422,000

Configuration: 3-1-1

Land Size: 680 sqm

Location: Western Sydney

Deposit: $84,400

Capital Expenses to purchase property at 10 % Deposits	
Purchase Price	$422,000
Loan amount required	$379,800
Deposits at 10 %	$42,200
Stamp duty	$14,500
Legal Expenses	$1,200
Building and pest inspections reports	$600
LMI	$9,370
Total	**$67,870**

Expenses	Weekly ($)	Monthly ($)	Annually ($)
Council rates	$30.77	$133.33	$1,600.00
Strata Fees	-	-	-
Water rates	$17.31	$75.00	$900.00
Building / Landlord insurance	$32.69	$141.67	$1,700
Management fees	$13.60	$58.93	$707.20
Mortgage Repayments	$306.76	$1329.30	$15951,60
Estimated Totals	**$410.13**	**$1738.23**	**$20,858.80**

Estimated Income			
Lower Rent	$340.00	$1473.33	$17,680.00
Higher Rent	$380.00	$1646.67	$19,760.00

Estimated cash flow before any tax considerations			
Lower Rent	$61.13	-$264.60	-$3178.80
Higher Rent	$21.13	-$91.57	-1,088.80

Property 3 happened in 2015.

I found property 3 in Western Sydney. I purchased that house as a planned move to repeat the same thing that I did with property 1: build a granny flat at the back, because I could again boost my overall income with the rental income.

Since my borrowing capacity was limited, I didn't go for high-end property. I did a bit more research for property 3 with the knowledge I gained from property 1 and 2. This time, I was confident, and I negotiated better.

I still remembered the property had an open inspection on a Saturday afternoon. I just hanged out with the agent until 7 p.m. I followed him to his office and told him that I wanted to purchase this. I presented my offer.

This was the time when people were actually more confident in buying after the global crisis. There were more than 60 people lined up for this property.

Because in 2015, lots of people wanted to build a Granny flat, everyone wanted to do the same thing for the second income. It was tough competition, but luckily, I knew the tactics to play around with the conditions.

My offer was accepted. The deposit of $84,000 was from savings.

Property 3 was purchased. I decided to build property

4 (a granny flat). But there was a rule that within five years, one cannot build two dwellings as a builder.

What's the next solution?

I encouraged my wife to get the builder's license, and then we built it using her license.

Property 4 (Granny flat- 3 bedrooms)

Year purchased: 2015

Purchase Price: $85,000

Configuration: 3-1-1

Land Size: 680sqm

Location: Western Sydney

Construction Costs: $85,000

Capital Expenses to purchase property at 20 % Deposits	
Purchase Price	$85,000
Loan amount required	-
Deposits at 20 %	-
Stamp duty	-
Legal Expenses	-
Building and pest inspections reports	-
Buffer	-
Total	$85,000

Expenses	Weekly ($)	Monthly ($)	Annually ($)
Council rates	-	-	-
Strata Fees	-	-	-
Water rates	-	-	-
Building / Landlord insurance	$7.60	$32.92	$395
Management fees	$23.20	$100.53	$1206.40
Mortgage Repayments	-	-	-
Estimated Totals	$30.80	$133.45	$1601.40
Estimated Income			
Lower Rent	$290.00	$1256.67	$15,080.00
Higher Rent	$310.00	$1343.33	$16,120.00
Estimated cash flow before any tax considerations			
Lower Rent	$259.20	$1,123.22	$13,478.60
Higher Rent	$279.20	$1209.88	$14,518.60

I did exactly what I did for my property 2 (Granny flat). The only difference was hiring a property manager to get quality tenants. The painful lesson I learnt: not to get tenants from Gumtree. It was not the best process to properly screen tenants.

My borrowing capacity was an issue to build a property portfolio now. It took me 3 years to get my 5th property.

I was speaking to different brokers and the second most important lesson in this property journey was to get the right broker. He or she should be an investment-savvy broker who could help you build a solid portfolio. The key thing here is to buy a property strategically so that you can get the next one.

You can't buy a million-dollar property first. Why? Because you're going to max out your borrowing capacity. This is one of the blunders that I observe in many new investors.

My 5th property taught me everything about the order of buying properties. And sequencing your order is crucial and that's exactly what I'm doing for my clients now.

Smart Move!

I Built a Granny Flat in Western Sydney for Just $85K!

Property 5

Year purchased: 2018

Purchase Price: $158,000

Configuration: 3-1-1

Land Size: townhouse, 230 sqm

Location: Brisbane, QLD

Deposit: $31,600

Capital Expenses to purchase property at 20 % Deposits	
Purchase Price	$158,000
Loan amount required	$126,400
Deposits at 20 %	$31,600
Stamp duty	$4,700
Legal Expenses	$1,500
Building and pest inspections reports	$500
Buffer	
Total	$38,300

Expenses	Weekly ($)	Monthly ($)	Annually ($)
Council rates	$30.77	$133.33	$1,600.00
Strata Fees	$65.77	$285.00	$3,420.00
Water rates	$26.92	$116.67	$1,400.00
Building / Landlord insurance	$7.60	$32.92	$395.00
Management fees	$16.20	$70.20	$842.40
Mortgage Repayments	$116.43	$504.55	$6,054.56
Estimated Totals	$263.69	$1,142.66	$13,711.96
Estimated Income			
Lower Rent	$270.00	$1,170.00	$14,040.00
Higher Rent	$280.00	$1,213.11	$14,560.00
Estimated cash flow before any tax considerations			
Lower Rent	$6.31	$27.34	$328.04
Higher Rent	$16.31	$70.67	$848.04

This was my first interstate investment. People thought I was crazy. Back then, QLD was not a popular place to invest. Prices were cheap though.

I knew the most important question to ask my broker. "What is my borrowing capacity and I don't want to max it out. I want to use only half of the borrowing capacity so that I can keep the other half to continue borrowing more."

My borrowing capacity at this stage was about $300,000. Buying a property with a purchase price of $150,000 was the ideal way. While investing and building a property portfolio, I already had future plans of building my dream house. With my remaining borrowing capacity, I could buy land in Sydney.

At this junction, I had 3 big questions in my mind:

1) Where can I buy affordable properties?

2) Where can I get the highest rental yield?

3) Where can I buy land in Sydney so that I can build my dream house?

Confidence was my superpower, I would say. My mind kept constantly thinking about "What's next?"

If property was a game, I was playing it well. Not emotionally but logically.

Buying an interstate property was indeed a nerve-wracking moment for me. I spoke to my agent 5 times. I requested a video walk through. It was the start of the iPhone, but there weren't many quality videos. The agent used his SLR camera and sent the video clips through Yahoo Mail. The property looked good.

I still remembered the conversation. The agent asked, "What do you think about the property?"

Without any emotions, I replied "Yeah, it looks nice."

And I continued, "Ok, let's go ahead with this."

Huge Risk. That was a huge risk.

I did not visit the Brisbane property (property 5). I did not go there. I did not send any friends to check it out. I just took the decisions over the phone and settled on that property. And back then, the interest rates started coming down a little in 2016.

My career was progressing well. I was also focused on increasing my income so that I could get better loans from the bank. My wife was working, and we were planning our finances to fund subsequent properties.

"What else can I do to increase our incomes? And what can I do next?"

These questions gave me more confidence about property investment.

Brisbane Bound!

My First Interstate Property Snagged for $158K!

Property 6

Year purchased: 2018

Purchase Price: $335,000

Configuration: 3-1-1

Land Size: 430 sqm

Location: Gold Coast, QLD

Deposit: $67,000

Capital Expenses to purchase property at 20 % Deposits	
Purchase Price	$335.000
Loan amount required	$268,000
Deposits at 20 %	$67,000
Stamp duty	$10,150
Legal Expenses	$1,500
Building and pest inspections reports	$600
Buffer	-
Total	$79,250

Expenses	Weekly ($)	Monthly ($)	Annually ($)
Council rates	$28.85	$125.00	$1,500.00
Strata Fees	-	-	-
Water rates	$26.92	$116.67	$1,400.00
Building / Landlord insurance	$19.23	$83.33	$1,000
Management fees	$30.40	$131.73	$1580.80
Mortgage Repayments	$246.87	$1069.77	$12,837.20
Estimated Totals	$352.27	$1526.50	$18,318.00

Estimated Income			
Lower Rent	$380.00	$1646.67	$19,760.00
Higher Rent	$420.00	$1,820.00	$21,840.00

Estimated cash flow before any tax considerations			
Lower Rent	$27.73	$120.17	$1,442.00
Higher Rent	$67.73	$293.50	$3,522.00

I bought property 6 on the Gold Coast. This was a similar process to property 5. I'd built quite a good rapport with sales agents and property managers. I requested a property manager to inspect this property. By now, I was able to understand the numbers. I was able to understand why I should buy a property in a particular area with more detailed analysis, not only about the market, but also about a specific property. The fundamental thing was building equity.

My confidence was boosted when I bought property 6 in Gold Coast. Three reasons again which I always emphasise

1) Why am I buying this property now?

2) How does this help me get my next one?

3) How would this property perform in the next 5 or 10 years?

Logical analysis, zero emotions.

Right now, you might be thinking, "How did you get the confidence to learn and execute on your own, especially for interstate investments?"

Honestly, I was hesitant in the beginning to go interstate.

But I always ask myself the big WHY question.

My thoughts were:

Why am I doing this?

Do I want to work full-time all my life?

Is there a way where I can become my own bank with consistent cash flow no matter what happens in the world?

In order to do that, I have to rely on property investments. I have to buy more properties. Not just one, but multiple properties.

And I don't need to work for all these mortgages. My tenants would pay the mortgage. Here comes the knowledge about debt. In schools, we are taught that debts are bad. We're culturally trained that 'no debt means more peace'. Even our elders and parents used to tell us that life without debt is the best.

However, the concept of debt is not what we think it is.

Debts can be good if you manage them in the right way. You don't blindly borrow money and waste it on liabilities or get credit cards to be trapped in debts.

Always correlate good debt with assets. You use debt to build assets.

If I have a debt of $1,400 from the bank and the tenant pays $1,300, it is not a debt.

What am I doing then?

This is leveraging money from the bank and the

tenants.

I understood leveraging, I understood debt, I understood how the tax works because tax is very complex in Australia.

By then I had developed a system and I was resourceful. I was not relying on anyone but myself. This massive confidence prompted me to make decisions very quickly, without any hesitations.

Why?

Because for years, I built that system. The list in my system was: What will be the rent? What will be the depreciation? What will be out of pocket expenses? What will be the tax savings?

These calculated risks helped me boost my confidence.

And then I never look back.

In my mind, you would be thinking,

"Oh Bharat, there are 6 properties now. I'm sure you have maintenance issues and tenant problems and a lot more issues, right? Is it worth it?"

If you buy a $400,000 property which is growing at 10%, that is $40,000 a year. And if I have to hold a property for $400 a month, it's $5,000 from your pocket. If you do the maths,

$40,000-$5000= $35,000, I'm still making money.

Gold Coast Jackpot!

Bought for $335K, but Now Worth $680K!

A Dream Home, My Dream Home

Property 7: My dream home

Year purchased: 2016-2018

Purchase Price: $860,000

Configuration: 5 beds, media, 3 baths, two kitchens, double garage

Land Size: 400sqm

Location: Western Sydney

Deposit: $172,000

When I was buying property number 5, I purchased a piece of land in Sydney. I already planned ahead. Back then, land was expensive (even now). But I bought in a place where land was at an affordable price. Less stamp duty on land. And then when the land was registered, I started building.

When you have land, your borrowing capacity has gone.

To avoid that, I invested in Brisbane (property 5) to buy an affordable property which would not max out my borrowing capacity.

What happens if I max out my borrowing capacity? I won't be able to buy my property 7 (my dream home).

You see how careful planning plays a role in building a property portfolio.

When my home construction started in Sydney, I didn't need to worry about my borrowing capacity. And for this property 7, my deposit was $172,000.

That was equity and savings. And equity from the previous properties I was holding.

Some people are sceptical of taking equity out from one property because there would be a new loan on the property that you extracted equity from. Some people might think "Why do I want to take a new loan and add more debt?"

As long as you invest in a property which is growing, you're going to make more money. Most of the people do not have the right education about property.

This is the property mortgage and the debt. They never think about the debt and inflation. That's where you will make more money from property.

And your debt becomes irrelevant in the next 10 years. Why? Because as long as you can keep good debt going, your hard-earned money will make more money for you.

It's all about educating you.

Your next question might be "If properties have

grown so much, why not sell those properties to enjoy the cash profits?"

Let me tell you a little secret about myself: I don't like selling my properties and I will never sell any of my properties in the future.

I moved into my dream house in 2018 as it took about 2 years to be completed. Once I had a Principal Place of Residence (PPOR), my borrowing capacity was affected. Why? Because there was no income generated from PPOR.

However, that didn't stop me from buying the next few properties.

Dream Home Secured!

My Forever Home in Western Sydney!

No Stopping: Properties 8, 9 and 10

Property 8

Year purchased: 2019

Purchase Price: $50,000

Configuration: 1-1 Studio

Land Size: 85sqm

Location: Cairns, QLD

Deposit: $50,000

Capital Expenses to purchase property at 20 % Deposit	
Purchase Price	$50,000
Loan amount required	-
Deposits at 20 %	-
Stamp duty	$7,50
Legal Expenses	$1,400
Building and pest inspections reports	$450
Buffer	
Total	$52,600

Expenses	Weekly ($)	Monthly ($)	Annually ($)
Council rates	$49.04	$212.50	$2,550.00
Strata Fees	$78.54	$340.33	$4,084.00
Water rates	-	-	-
Building / Landlord insurance	-	-	-
Management fees	$16.00	$69.33	$832.00
Mortgage Repayments	-	-	-
Estimated Totals	$143.58	$622.17	$7,466.00

Estimated Income			
Lower Rent	$200.00	$866.67	$10,400.00
Higher Rent	$220.00	$953.33	$11,440.00

Estimated cash flow before any tax considerations			
Lower Rent	$56.42	$244.50	$2,934.00
Higher Rent	$76.42	$331.17	$3,974.00

Steal of a Deal!

First Budget Property in QLD for Just $50K!

Property 9

Year purchased: 2020

Purchase Price: $65,000

Configuration: 1-1 Studio

Land Size: 70sqm

Location: Brisbane, QLD

Deposit: $65,000

Capital Expenses to purchase property at 20 % Deposits	
Purchase Price	$65,000
Loan amount required	-
Deposits at 20 %	-
Stamp duty	$1,100
Legal Expenses	$1,400
Building and pest inspections reports	$450
Buffer	-
Total	$67,950

Expenses	Weekly ($)	Monthly ($)	Annually ($)
Council rates	$38.46	$166.67	$2,000.00
Strata Fees	$182.69	$791.67	$9,500.00
Water rates	$25.00	$108.33	$1,300.00
Landlord insurance	7.60	$32.92	$395.00
Management fees	$28.00	$121.33	$1,456.00
Mortgage Repayments	-	-	-
Estimated Totals	$281.75	$1,220.92	$14,651.00

Estimated Income			
Lower Rent	$400.00	$1,733.33	$20,800.00
Higher Rent	$420.00	$1,820.00	$21,840.00

Estimated cash flow before any tax considerations			
Lower Rent	$118.25	$512.42	$6,149.00
Higher Rent	$138.25	$599.08	$7,189.00

Rental Goldmine!

Bought for $65K, Now Renting at $590/Week!

Property 10

Year purchased: 2020

Purchase Price: $65,000

Configuration: 1-1 Studio

Land Size: 70sqm

Location: Brisbane, QLD

Deposit: $65,000

Capital Expenses to purchase property at 20 % Deposits	
Purchase Price	$65,000
Loan amount required	-
Deposits at 20 %	-
Stamp duty	$1,100
Legal Expenses	$1,400
Building and pest inspections reports	$450
Buffer	-
Total	**$67,950**

Expenses	Weekly ($)	Monthly ($)	Annually ($)
Council rates	$38.46	$166.67	$2,000.00
Strata Fees	$182.69	$791.67	$9,500.00
Water rates	$25.00	$108.33	$1,300.00
Landlord insurance	7.60	$32.92	$395.00
Management fees	$28.00	$121.33	$1,456.00
Mortgage Repayments	-	-	-
Estimated Totals	**$281.75**	**$1,220.92**	**$14,651.00**

Estimated Income			
Lower Rent	$400.00	$1,733.33	$20,800.00
Higher Rent	$420.00	$1,820.00	$21,840.00

Estimated cash flow before any tax considerations			
Lower Rent	$118.25	$512.42	$6,149.00
Higher Rent	$138.25	$599.08	$7,189.00

I purchased properties 8, 9 and 10 to boost my borrowing capacity. Every property was bought with a purpose. I invest my money to make more money because I don't like cash, I like cash flow.

At this point, one has to remember that increasing your income (career/job) is equally important. As much as rental income is paramount, your income plays a major part in ensuring you can keep borrowing. Property investment is one thing, asking your employer or boss to increase your pay or seek better opportunities is another thing.

Do your job well. Learn as much as you can. Show them you're a valuable player in the team. When I was working as an IT manager, every year I asked my boss for a 10% increase. Jokingly, I would say if I didn't get a 10% increase, I would find a new job. He would laugh and reply to me with "Why do you keep asking for a raise every year?"

"Brother, because I need more money. I am more than happy to work more."

Employers know that if you're a valuable contributor, they would do anything to retain you. So, play the game.

Meanwhile, my wife launched her childcare business from our home and that generated a substantial income too. With a full-time job, one could go up to 3 or 4 properties. After that, you need to be doing something bigger than the norm.

Hitting 10 properties, a milestone and a habit

The hunger didn't stop. A positive hunger.

The hunger drive kept me on the move:

What was my next milestone after property 10?

How can I overcome borrowing capacity issues?

What can I do next?

What kind of property do I need to buy?

I spent 10 years educating myself to buy only 10 properties. If I can buy 10 more properties in maybe a lot less than 10 years, how would that be?

I became very aggressive after 10 properties. As long as I found the right property with careful analysis, I bought it. Sometimes, it could be looking at a property in the morning and signing the contract on the same day. It became more like a healthy obsession. Because I'd built the system and the right resources, I had the right mortgage broker in my team. I had the right solicitor. I had everything right. By this time, it was 2019 and online information became more accessible.

Double Digits!

Celebrating My 10th Property Purchase!

Property 11

Year purchased: 2020

Purchase Price: $491,750

Configuration: side by side duplex. 3-1-1- one side, 2-1-1 other side

Land Size: 742 sqm

Location: Brisbane, QLD

Deposit: $98,350

Capital Expenses to purchase property at 20 % Deposits	
Purchase Price	$491,750
Loan amount required	$393,400
Deposits at 20 %	$98,350
Stamp duty	$15,638
Legal Expenses	$1,600
Building and pest inspections reports	$600
Buffer	-
Total	$116,188

Expenses	Weekly ($)	Monthly ($)	Annually ($)
Council rates	$32.69	$141.67	$1,700.00
Strata Fees	-	-	-
Water rates	$25.00	$108.33	$1,300.00
Building / Landlord insurance	$32.69	$141.67	$1,700.00
Management fees	$44.10	$191.10	$2,293.20
Mortgage Repayments	$287.48	$1,245.77	$14,949.20
Estimated Totals	$421.97	$1,828.53	$21,942.40

Estimated Income			
Lower Rent	$630.00	$2,730.00	$32,760.00
Higher Rent	$680.00	$2,946.67	$35,360.00

Estimated cash flow before any tax considerations			
Lower Rent	$208.03	$901.47	$10,817.60
Higher Rent	$258.03	$1,18.13	$13,417.60

First Duplex Deal!

Secured for $491,750 in Brisbane!

Property 12

Year purchased: 2021

Purchase Price: $60,000

Configuration: Studio 1-1

Land Size: 80sqm

Location: Cairns QLD

Deposit: $60,000

Capital Expenses to purchase property at 20 % Deposits	
Purchase Price	$60,000
Loan amount required	-
Deposits at 20 %	-
Stamp duty	$900
Legal Expenses	$1,400
Building and pest inspections reports	$450
Buffer	-
Total	$62,750

Expenses	Weekly ($)	Monthly ($)	Annually ($)
Council rates	$49.04	$212.50	$2,550.00
Strata Fees & Insurance	$78.54	$340.33	$4,084.00
Water rates	-	-	-
Building / Landlord insurance	-	-	-
Management fees	$17.60	$76.27	$915.20
Mortgage Repayments	-	-	-
Estimated Totals	$145.18	$629.10	$7,549.20

Estimated Income			
Lower Rent	$220.00	$953.33	$11,440.00
Higher Rent	$240.00	$1,040.00	$12,480.00

Estimated cash flow before any tax considerations			
Lower Rent	$74.82	$324.23	$3,890.80
Higher Rent	$94.82	$410.90	$4,930.80

If I could pick up something a bit smaller at this price, I could make double the money in a shorter period of time. That was why I picked up that property. Also, at the back of my mind, I did not want to buy 10 properties. I wanted to buy many more properties.

Property 13

Year purchased: 2021

Purchase Price: $107,000

Configuration: Villa - 2-1-1

Land Size: 170sqm

Where: Brisbane, QLD

Deposit: $21,400

Capital Expenses to purchase property at 20 % Deposits	
Purchase Price	$107,000
Loan amount required	-
Deposits at 20 %	-
Stamp duty	$2,170
Legal Expenses	$1,600
Building and pest inspections reports	$450
Buffer	-
Total	$111,220

Expenses	Weekly ($)	Monthly ($)	Annually ($)
Council rates	$38.46	$166.67	$2,000.00
Strata Fees & Insurance	$182.69	$791.67	$9,500.00
Water rates	$25.00	$108.33	$1,300.00
Landlord insurance	$7.60	$32.92	$395.00
Management fees	$33.60	$145.60	$1,747.20
Mortgage Repayments			
Estimated Totals	$287.35	$1,245.18	$14,942.20

Estimated Income			
Lower Rent	$480.00	$2,080.00	$24,960.00
Higher Rent	$500.00	$2,166.67	$26,000.00

Estimated cash flow before any tax considerations			
Lower Rent	$192.65	$834.82	$10,017.80
Higher Rent	$212.65	$921.48	$11,067.80

So far, I have been buying in Queensland (QLD). Why? The rent was great in QLD. Buying cheap properties was only one factor. Not all cheap properties would grow. That's why I relied on my system which has 30 data factors. With the system I built, I could easily analyse a property within a few minutes, and place an offer.

Property 14

Year purchased: 2021

Purchase Price: $110,000

Configuration: Villa 2-1-1

Land Size: 150sqm

Location: Brisbane QLD

Deposit: $22,000

My borrowing capacity started improving because of the low interest in 2021. I received more rental income. At this point with a structured strategy, I wanted to improve cash flow so that I could keep building my portfolio.

I didn't want to stop at 10 or 15 properties. Things became more interesting. As I explored the New South Wales market in 2021, Covid was at its peak.

Property 15

Year purchased: 2021

Purchase Price: $96,250

Configuration: House - 3-1-1

Land Size: 597 sqm

Location: NSW Regional

Deposit: $19,250

Capital Expenses to purchase property at 20 % Deposits	
Purchase Price	$96,250
Loan amount required	$77,000
Deposits at 20 %	$19,750
Stamp duty	$1,534
Legal Expenses	$1,500
Building and pest inspections reports	$600
Buffer	-
Total	**$22,884**

Expenses	Weekly ($)	Monthly ($)	Annually ($)
Council rates	$25.00	$108.00	$1,300.00
Strata Fees	-	-	-
Water rates	$9.62	$41.67	$500.00
Building insurance	$21.15	$91.67	$1,100.00
Management fees	$23.20	$100.53	$1,206.40
Mortgage Repayments	$45.02	$195.07	$2,340.80
Estimated Totals	**$123.98**	**$537.27**	**$6,447.20**

Estimated Income			
Lower Rent	$290.00	$1,256.67	$15,080.00
Higher Rent	$310.00	$2,343.33	$16,120.00

Estimated cash flow before any tax considerations			
Lower Rent	$166.02	$719.40	$8,632.80
Higher Rent	$186.02	$806.07	$9,672.80

Property 15 was from the Department of Public Housing. They were selling two to three properties. And I thought "oh, let me grab something if I can."

The kitchen was ruined, the bedroom had many maintenance/repair issues, the bathroom needed work and there were broken tiles. This house was on auction. And I bought it.

On the other hand, I was slightly nervous too because this house had termite issues. See, I am a human being. I won't say that I would never ever get anxious about property purchases. Properties with high risk as such do question my belief system. But I don't sit and complain. I look for solutions.

I had to spend about $25,000-$30,000 to fix all the issues. I already built two granny flats and I had knowledge of building granny flats and how tradesmen work. I was able to clear the termite affected timber in the house.

Building rapport with sales agents was a key factor

Apart from many variables and factors, having a good relationship and rapport with sales agents make the journey a better one. Over the years, I've built some good connections with the agents. Scaling your property portfolio becomes easy when you have made that connection.

When I first started, no sales agent picked up the call. I did it consistently. Every week, I called them. I spoke to them about their interests and made genuine friendships. It took time, weeks, months and years.

Bad Tenants and Threats

I had an unpleasant experience with one of my tenants. There was this lady who dumped baby napkins down the toilet flush system. The toilet flushing system was blocked. Immediately, I had to call the plumber to replace the system. But the tenant was unhappy that if I didn't install a fence around the house, she would burn down the house. That literally devastated me. Not paying rent was one issue. What if she really burnt the house down? I was hoping and praying hard that she didn't do anything crazy. I found the right property agent and then we safely and quickly asked her to leave the property. Thanks to the amazing property manager!

Lesson learnt: To be proactive and regularly do checks on the properties. I also developed a good relationship with the property managers as well. Every three months we receive the reports and we analyse them.

Is property investment stressful? No.

It's managing the people that can be a challenge.

Fixer-Upper Win!

How I Grabbed a Termite-Damaged Home for
Just $96,250 at Auction!

Chapter 5

Don't Listen to People Who Aren't Savvy Investors! (Property 16-30)

By now, readers may have this question: How much do you have to spend to hold each property?

Right now, my annual rental income (for all 30 properties) is $600,000. I am paying about $27,000 in interest. For each property, I would say I spend about $600/month as holding expenses.

If you're earning $100k or even 90k, you can still get on the property journey. With your partner's income, you can do more. It's all about buying the right properties in the right order which is very important. You can see that I don't buy a million-dollar property. It is always in the mid-range.

People are worried about high interest rates. Buy when you can. When interest rates come down, it is going to be a game changer for investors, because you can borrow more. You don't have to spend too much on holding expenses. And whatever you spend, you can claim back from tax. Yes, $500 per month as a holding cost is an expense. That is going to be $6,000 per year. At the same time, if your 400k property is growing at 10%, that is $40,000. You're making more money than you're spending. Look at the bigger picture. Look further ahead.

That's how I'm educating my clients in my buyer's agency at Cashflow Properties. I've closed 200 deals in 2 years of launching my company with the bigger picture and long-term vision for clients.

And the most important part of the journey: If I had built my dream home (property 7) in the first place instead of building a property portfolio, would I have achieved 30 properties?

The answer is definitely NO.

I would probably be working all my life just to pay off that one dream home. It would no longer be a pleasant dream, probably a nightmare.

My first house (property 1) was a simple home. I didn't go for any million dollar or 2-million-dollar luxury home first. It was a simple 3-bedroom house. When there were guests, and they used one of the rooms, I had to sleep on the couch.

After building a property portfolio that gave me confidence and cash flow, I could build my dream home (property 7). Now there are more features that I could add to it: A massive master bedroom, 2 rooms for the kids, big guest rooms, 2 kitchen areas and a good-sized prayer room.

It is literally my dream home because I worked hard for it by building a back plan (financial wealth and freedom).

Another lesson in this journey: Your first home is never your forever home. Even if you want to get your own home, go for something simple and functional. Stay there for a few years, work hard and invest in the right properties. Gradually aim for a better home. Think of the next step in a strategic way. Start buying under your personal names, and then you can think of trust structures. Work with professionals to get you on the property journey smoothly.

As already mentioned earlier, every property you buy (for your own stay or investment) should have a meaningful purpose. And you get clarity by asking these 3 questions:

1. Why am I buying this property?

2. What am I trying to achieve in the next 3 or 6 months or even 5 or 10 years?

3. What will be the next property after buying this one?

Very simple, right? It's like a chess game. You need to know the opponents, then depending on what move they make, you need to think of the next step.

Every property I purchase, I only think of three things: equity purpose, cashflow purpose or cosmetic renovation purpose. Depending on that, I would structure my property. Is it best to buy under my name, joint name, and company name or trust name? And everything has both pros and cons. You learn to evaluate and make informed decisions.

In 2021, I bought 6 properties in total.

Property 16

Year purchased: 2021

Purchase Price: $290,000

Configuration: House 3-1-1

Land Size: 646sqm

Location: QLD Regional

Deposit: $58,000

Capital Expenses to purchase property at 20 % Deposits	
Purchase Price	$290,000
Loan amount required	$232,000
Deposits at 20 %	$58,000
Stamp duty	$10,000
Legal Expenses	$2,000
Building and pest inspections reports	$600
Buffer	-
Total	$70,600

Expenses	Weekly ($)	Monthly ($)	Annually ($)
Council rates	$61.54	$266.67	$3,200
Strata Fees	-	-	-
Water rates	$7.69	$33.33	$400.00
Building insurance	$32.69	$141.67	$1,700.00
Management fees	$27.20	$117.87	$1,414.40
Mortgage Repayments	$135.63	$587.73	$7,052.80
Estimated Totals	$264.75	$1,147.27	$13,767.20
Estimated Income			
Lower Rent	$340.00	$1,473.33	$17,680.00
Higher Rent	$380.00	$1,646.67	$19,760.00
Estimated cash flow before any tax considerations			
Lower Rent	$75.25	$326.07	$3,912.80
Higher Rent	$115.25	$499.00	$5,992.80

Incredible Find!

I Snagged This Regional QLD Property for
Just $290K During COVID-19.

Property 17

Year purchased: 2021

Purchase Price: $210,000

Configuration: House 3-1-1

Land Size: 569 sqm

Location: QLD Regional

Deposit: $42,000

Capital Expenses to purchase property at 20 % Deposits	
Purchase Price	$210,000
Loan amount required	$168,000
Deposits at 20 %	$42,000
Stamp duty	$6,000
Legal Expenses	$2,000
Building and pest inspections reports	$600
Buffer	-
Total	$50,600

Expenses	Weekly ($)	Monthly ($)	Annually ($)
Council rates	$65.38	$283.33	$3,400.00
Strata Fees	-	-	-
Water rates	-	-	-
Building insurance	$33.94	$147.08	$1,765.00
Management fees	$24.00	$104.00	$1,248.00
Mortgage Repayments	$98.22	$425.60	$5,107.20
Estimated Totals	$221.54	$960.02	$11,520.20

Estimated Income			
Lower Rent	$300.00	$1,300.00	$15,600.00
Higher Rent	$320.00	$1,386.67	$16,640.00

Estimated cash flow before any tax considerations			
Lower Rent	$78.46	$339.98	$4,079.80
Higher Rent	$98.46	$426.65	$5,119.80

It was Covid time. All of us were trapped in our homes. I took advantage of the time at home. I kept building my relationships with sales agents and property managers. It was the best time to buy when others were fearful.

I still remember that chaotic period: The first case of Covid was detected in Australia. I was in India for the holidays. Immediately I flew from India back to Australia and the whole world was in panic mode. There was a lockdown. Then I heard that the real estate agency couldn't open the door because of the Covid restrictions.

There were some sellers who were desperate. The general mindset of people: Market crash and this was the worst time to buy.

I thought if I took advantage of this period, I could accumulate more properties. And I did buy more affordable properties. Getting tenants was not difficult, except for one of my properties. They wanted to move out of their parents' home. After that, my property was vacant for some time because of the restriction. Eventually, we found a tenant.

My whole focus was not worrying about expenses, but: "What can I do next?" "How can I increase my income so that I can go and buy more, right?"

Initially, for my first 3 or 4 properties, yes, I was terrified. Once I started investing interstate, my confidence level went to another level.

Timing is Everything!
I Bought This Townsville Gem for $210K
at the Market's Lowest Point in 2021.

Property 18 and 19
(Duplex- 2 separate units)

Year purchased: 2022

Purchase Price: $208,000

Configuration: Duplex, 2-1-1 each side

Land Size: 768 sqm

Location: QLD Regional

Deposit: $41,600

Capital Expenses to purchase property at 20 % Deposits	
Purchase Price	$208,000
Loan amount required	$166,400
Deposits at 20 %	$41,600
Stamp duty	$7,088
Legal Expenses	$2,200
Building and pest inspections reports	$600
Buffer	-
Total	$51,488

Expenses	Weekly ($)	Monthly ($)	Annually ($)
Council rates	$67.31	$291.67	$3,500.00
Strata Fees	-	-	-
Water rates	-	-	-
Building insurance	$32.69	$141.67	$1,700.00
Management fees	$27.20	$117.87	$1,414.40
Mortgage Repayments	$214.40	$929.07	$11,148.80
Estimated Totals	$341.60	$1,480.27	$17,763.20

Estimated Income			
Lower Rent	$340.00	$1,473.33	$17,680.00
Higher Rent	$380.00	$1,646.67	$19,760.00

Estimated cash flow before any tax considerations			
Lower Rent	$1.60	-$6.93	-$83.20
Higher Rent	$38.40	$166.40	$1,996.80

Properties 18 and 19 were a duplex. In my portfolio, there are many types of properties such as houses, duplexes and villas. As I've mentioned earlier-each property should fall under one of these categories:

1) Am I buying for growth?

2) Am I buying to get equity?

3) Am I buying to renovate and refinance?

When I buy a property, it should lead me to the next level of borrowing capacity. When I bought properties 18 and 19 which were a duplex, there were two separate rental incomes.

There is one type of property which I would never purchase: a high-rise apartment.

A Steal!

I Secured This Affordable Duplex for
Only $208K During COVID-19!

Property 20

Year purchased: 2022

Purchase Price: $342,500

Configuration: House 4-2-2

Land Size: 800sqm

Location: QLD

Deposit: $68,500

Capital Expenses to purchase property at 20 % Deposits	
Purchase Price	$342.500
Loan amount required	$274.000
Deposits at 20 %	$68,500
Stamp duty	$11,435
Legal Expenses	$2,000
Building and pest inspections reports	$600
Buffer	-
Total	**$82,535**

Expenses	Weekly ($)	Monthly ($)	Annually ($)
Council rates	$57.69	$250.00	$3,000
Strata Fees	-	-	-
Water rates	$15.38	$66.67	$800.00
Building insurance	$12.62	$54.67	$656.00
Management fees	$26.60	$115.27	$1,383.20
Mortgage Repayments	$26.60	$115.27	$1,383.20
Estimated Totals	**$272.48**	**$1,180.73**	**$14,168.80**

Estimated Income			
Lower Rent	$380.00	$1,646.67	$19,760.00
Higher Rent	$480.00	$2,080.00	$24,960.00

Estimated cash flow before any tax considerations			
Lower Rent	$107.52	$465.93	$5,591.20
Higher Rent	$207.52	$899.27	$10,791.20

This was a bigger piece of land, 800 sqm. Regional Queensland was an interesting region. I could get a good size piece of land and a property with a strong rental yield compared to other states. After exhausting my purchasing power in metro cities like Brisbane and Gold Coast, I went to regional areas. I picked up at the right cycle, so those regional areas had not grown too much for the last few years.

After the pandemic, people moved to these beautiful seaside locations, where I bought. When they started moving to these areas, growth happened. When I bought in 2022, those houses were still in the 250k-280k. Now in 2024, it has doubled almost. So back in 2022, I took advantage of those cheap properties. The main reason for QLD was the diverse economy and job opportunities, which drove up house prices.

And every time you buy a property, there is always a little bit of risk. Even with all the calculations and analysis, there are a few things which aren't under our control.

When I chose regional QLD, there was a little bit of risk. Since this was my 20th property, I could take a risk. That was how I got property 21 and 22.

How Sydney couple has 20 properties worth $7.5m

He arrived in Sydney with just two suitcases full of clothes – but now he owns 20 properties and is looking to buy more.

Property 21

Year purchased: 2022

Purchase Price: $260,000

Configuration: House 3-1-1

Land Size: 589sqm

Location: QLD Regional

Deposit: $52,000

Capital Expenses to purchase property at 20 % Deposits	
Purchase Price	$260,000
Loan amount required	$208,000
Deposits at 20 %	$52,000
Stamp duty	$7,525
Legal Expenses	$2,000
Building and pest inspections reports	$600
Buffer	-
Total	$62,125

Expenses	Weekly ($)	Monthly ($)	Annually ($)
Council rates	$46.15	$200.00	$2,400.00
Strata Fees	-	-	-
Water rates	$13.46	$58.33	$700.00
Building insurance	$12.50	$54.12	$650.00
Management fees	$30.40	$131.73	$1,580.80
Mortgage Repayments	$139.60	$604.93	$7,259.20
Estimated Totals	$242.12	$1,049.17	$12,590.00
Estimated Income			
Lower Rent	$380.00	$1,646.67	$19,760.00
Higher Rent	$400.00	$1,733.33	$20,800.00
Estimated cash flow before any tax considerations			
Lower Rent	$137.88	$597.50	$7,170.00
Higher Rent	$157.88	$684.17	$8,210.00

Auction Win!

I Grabbed This Distressed Property for
Just $260K During COVID-19.

Property 22

Year purchased: 2023

Purchase Price: $250,000

Configuration: house 4-2-2

Land Size: 672 sqm

Location: QLD Regional

Deposit: $50,000

Capital Expenses to purchase property at 20 % Deposits	
Purchase Price	$250,000
Loan amount required	$200,000
Deposits at 20 %	$50,000
Stamp duty	$7,935
Legal Expenses	$2,000
Building and pest inspections reports	$800
Buffer	
Total	$60,735

Expenses	Weekly ($)	Monthly ($)	Annually ($)
Council rates	$55.77	$241.67	$2,900.00
Strata Fees	-	-	-
Water rates	-	-	-
Building insurance	$14.42	$62.50	$750.00
Management fees	$28.00	$121.33	$1,456.00
Mortgage Repayments	$153.85	666.67	$8,000.00
Estimated Totals	**$252.04**	**$1,092.17**	**$13,106.00**
Lower Rent	$350.00	$1,516.67	$18,200.00
Higher Rent	$370.00	$1,603.33	$19,240.00

Estimated cash flow before any tax considerations			
Lower Rent	$97.96	$424.50	$5,094.00
Higher Rent	$117.96	$511.17	$6,134.00

For property 23, I bought it under a self-managed super fund (SMSF). Because I did not have enough funds as I had exhausted most of my borrowing capacity at that time. I've also launched my business 'cash flow properties'. And then there was only one solution: SMSF.

An Unbelievable Deal!

I Picked up This Regional QLD Duplex for Only $250K.

Property 23

Year purchased: 2023

Purchase Price: $260,000

Configuration: House 3-1-1

Land Size: 632sqm

Location: QLD Regional

Deposit: $52,000

Capital Expenses to purchase property at 20 % Deposits	
Purchase Price	$260.000
Loan amount required	$208.000
Deposits at 20 %	$52.000
Stamp duty	$7,525
Legal Expenses	$1,800
Building and pest inspections reports	$495
Buffer	-
Total	$61,820

Expenses	Weekly ($)	Monthly ($)	Annually ($)
Council rates	$67.31	$291.67	$3,500.00
Strata Fees	-	-	-
Water rates	-	-	-
Building insurance	$26.92	$116.67	$1,400.00
Management fees	$27.20	$117.87	$1,414.40
Mortgage Repayments	$360.69	$1,563.00	$18,756.00
Estimated Totals	$482.12	$2,089.20	$25,070.40

Estimated Income			
Lower Rent	$340.00	$1,473.33	$17,680.00
Higher Rent	$380.00	$1,646.67	$19,760.00

Estimated cash flow before any tax considerations			
Lower Rent	$142.12	-$615.87	$7,390.40
Higher Rent	$102.12	-$442.53	$5,310.40

My First SMSF Investment!

—I Locked in This Beauty for Just $260K!

Property 24

Year purchased: 2023

Purchase Price: $154,000

Configuration: Townhouse 3-1-1

Land Size: 324 sqm

Location: QLD Regional

Deposit: $30,400

Capital Expenses to purchase property at 20 % Deposits	
Purchase Price	$154,000
Loan amount required	$123,200
Deposits at 20 %	$30,800
Stamp duty	$3,815
Legal Expenses	$2,000
Building and pest inspections reports	$600
Buffer	-
Total	$37,215

Expenses	Weekly ($)	Monthly ($)	Annually ($)
Council rates	$57.69	$250.00	$3,000.00
Strata Fees	$45.88	$198.83	$2,386.00
Water rates	-	-	-
Landlord insurance	$7.60	$32.92	$395.00
Management fees	$26.40	$114.40	$1,372.80
Mortgage Repayments	$162.23	$703.00	$8,436.00
Estimated Totals	$299.80	$1,299.15	$15,589.80
Estimated Income			
Lower Rent	$330.00	$1,430.00	$17,160.00
Higher Rent	$380.00	$1,646.67	$19,760.00
Estimated cash flow before any tax considerations			
Lower Rent	$30.20	$130.85	$1,570.20
Higher Rent	$80.20	$347.52	$4,170.20

When I bought townhouses, there was a slight difference in the way I researched them. For property 24, the houses in this suburb were not ideal for my portfolio. It was expensive. But I knew that this suburb still had potential. What's the next best option? Townhouses.

The ratio between the owner-occupiers and investors should be right. I didn't want to invest in a place where there was a high demand for investors. I bought in a place where the demand for owners-occupiers was high. This meant that people who couldn't afford homes would start looking into townhouses and thus this would increase the value of them.

The houses then were about $400k-500k and had already grown too much. The townhouses were about $150k. This property I bought had some renovation potential. I spent around $5,000 to $7,000 to repair the bathroom. Thus, the property was sold at a cheaper price. I saw the potential and bought it. The valuation of the house was over $200k then. I made equity on the day of the purchase.

For the next few properties, I looked into Tasmania and Western Australia.

Another Smart Move!

I Secured my Second SMSF Property for Just $152K.

Property 25

Year purchased: 2023

Purchase Price: $350,000

Configuration: House 3-1-1

Land Size: 653sqm

Location: Tasmania

Deposit: $70,000

I started 'Cashflow Properties' in 2022. After launching my business, my borrowing capacity increased significantly. I was in a position to grow my portfolio from my business income as well.

Even up till today, I don't buy a million-dollar property as an investment. I would buy a property that would grow into a million-dollar property in 10 to 15 years' time. Even in your worst-case scenario, let's say you've lost your job, your rent can still cover most of the mortgage and expenses. Buy a property that would self-run during your difficult periods.

Breathtaking Tasmanian Property!

an absolute dream!

Property 26

Year purchased: 2022

Purchase Price: $450,000

Configuration: House 3-1-1

Land Size: 456 sqm

Location: Western Australia

Deposit: $90,000

The diversification happened because I had enough properties in Queensland and New South Wales. I just wanted to explore the options.

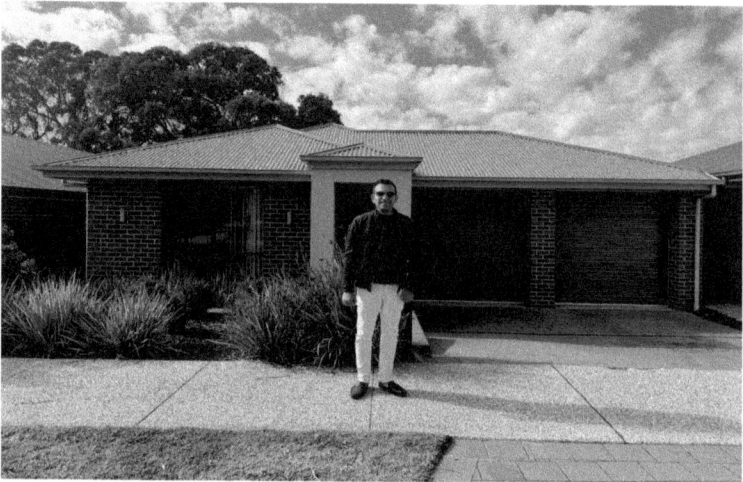

Fresh Investment!

Secured this Western Australia Property in 2022.

Property 27

Year purchased: 2023

Purchase Price: $390,000

Configuration: House -3-1-1

Land Size: 521sqm

Location: South Australia

Deposit: $78,000

Capital Expenses to purchase property at 20 % Deposits	
Purchase Price	$390,000
Loan amount required	$312,000
Deposits at 20 %	$78,000
Stamp duty	$15,830
Legal Expenses	$700
Building and pest inspections reports	$600
Buffer	-
Total	$95,130

Expenses	Weekly ($)	Monthly ($)	Annually ($)
Council rates	$26.92	$116.67	$1,400.00
Strata Fees	-	-	-
Water rates	$7.69	$33.33	$400.00
Building insurance	$15.38	$66.67	$800.00
Management fees	$33.60	$145.60	$1,747.20
Mortgage Repayments	$390.00	$1,690.00	$20.280.00
Estimated Totals	$473.60	$2,052.27	$24,627.20

Estimated Income			
Lower Rent	$420.00	$1,820.00	$21,840.00
Higher Rent	$440.00	$1,906.67	$22,880.00

Estimated cash flow before any tax considerations			
Lower Rent	$53.60	-$232.27	-$2787.20
Higher Rent	$33.60	-$145.60	-$1747.20

Property 28

Year purchased: 2023.

Purchase Price: $430,000

Configuration: House 3-1-1

Land Size: 342sqm

Location: South Australia

Deposit: $86,000

Capital Expenses to purchase property at 20 % Deposits	
Purchase Price	$430,000
Loan amount required	$344,000
Deposits at 20 %	$86,000
Stamp duty	$17,830
Legal Expenses	$700
Building and pest inspections reports	$600
Buffer	-
Total	$105,130

Expenses	Weekly ($)	Monthly ($)	Annually ($)
Council rates	$26.92	$116.67	$1,400.00
Strata Fees	-	-	-
Water rates	$7.69	$33.33	$400.00
Building insurance	$14.25	$61.75	$741.00
Management fees	$31.60	$136.93	$1,643.20
Mortgage Repayments	$463.08	$2006.67	$24,080.00
Estimated Totals	$543.54	$2,355.35	$28,264.20

Estimated Income			
Lower Rent	$395.00	$1,711.67	$20,540.00
Higher Rent	$420.00	$1,820.00	$21,840.00

Estimated cash flow before any tax considerations			
Lower Rent	$148.54	-$643.68	-$7,724.20
Higher Rent	$12.354	-$535.35	-$6,424.20

Diversification is one main reason to invest in different states. The other is land tax. I don't pay too much land tax on every single purchase.

Prime Pick in Adelaide!
Another Solid Addition to the Portfolio!

Property 29

Year purchased: 2023

Purchase Price: $630,000

Configuration: House 4-2-2

Land Size: 567 sqm

Location: Western Australia

Deposit: $126,000

Capital Expenses to purchase property at 20 % Deposits	
Purchase Price	$630,000
Loan amount required	$504,000
Deposits at 20 %	$126,000
Stamp duty	$23,940
Legal Expenses	$2000
Building and pest inspections reports	$600
Buffer	-
Total	**$152,540**

Expenses	Weekly ($)	Monthly ($)	Annually ($)
Council rates	$34.62	$150.00	$1,800.00
Strata Fees	-	-	-
Water rates	$22.83	$98.92	$1,187.00
Building insurance	$16.63	$72.08	$865.00
Management fees	$47.20	$204.53	$2,454.40
Mortgage Repayments	$649.38	$2,814.00	$33,768.00
Estimated Totals	**$770.66**	**$3,359.53**	**$40,074.40**
Estimated Income			
Lower Rent	$590.00	$2,556.67	$30,680.00
Higher Rent	$620.00	$2,686.67	$32,240.00
Estimated cash flow before any tax considerations			
Lower Rent	$180.66	-$782.87	-$9,394.40
Higher Rent	$150.66	-$652.87	-$7,834.40

Property 30

Year purchased: 2023

Purchase Price: $490,000

Configuration: Duplex, 2-1-1 each side

Land Size: 700m2

Location: Tasmania

Deposit: $98,000

Capital Expenses to purchase property at 20 % Deposits	
Purchase Price	$490,000
Loan amount required	$392,000
Deposits at 20 %	$98,000
Stamp duty	$17,822
Legal Expenses	$1,400
Building and pest inspections reports	$800
Buffer	-
Total	**$118,022**

Expenses	Weekly ($)	Monthly ($)	Annually ($)
Council rates	$26.92	$116.67	$1,400.00
`Strata Fees	-	-	-
Water rates	$7.69	$33.33	$400.00
Building insurance	$23.08	$100.00	$1,200.00
Management fees	$41.60	$180.27	$2,163.20
Mortgage Repayments	$527.69	$2,286.67	$27,440.00
Estimated Totals	$626.98	$2,716.93	$32,603.20

Estimated Income			
Lower Rent	$520.00	$2,253.33	$27,040.00
Higher Rent	$540.00	$2,340.00	$28,080.00

Estimated cash flow before any tax considerations			
Lower Rent	$106.98	-$463.50	-$5,563.20
Higher Rent	$86.98	-$376.93	-$4,523.20

Stunning Duplex in Tasmania!

Secured in 2023 and Worth Every Dollar!

Chapter 6

Think Big, Start Small

Building a portfolio of 30 properties and launching my buyer's agency business meant 2 things for me: My goals were clear, my objectives were clear, no confusion, no doubts, consistency was key, and I never gave up in any circumstances.

Sometimes intrusive thoughts would cross my mind: What if I lost my job or business? Or, if something happened to me physically or my health was affected severely?

Every single purchase taught me a backup plan. Every single property along the way had a challenge then I tried to think outside the box and find the solution.

No 1: Have a strong mindset, as long as you have a strong mindset of doing any tasks, anything can be done.

No 2: Then you have to break down the problems into simple tasks, and then try to do every single task.

No 3: Then you need to build a strategy. Once you decide something, you need to know how you are going to do it. Then you have to take action.

These are the three things I learned. And after 30 properties, I decided I didn't have to rely on any economy, systems, or interest rates.

I wanted to have my own bank.

New investors, you need to think outside your

backyard. If you are someone from Sydney or Melbourne at the age of 25 or 30, stop thinking of getting a million dollar home first. Change your mindset, develop your strategy. You can't achieve your dream home without proper strategy and proper investment.

My humble advice for any new investors regardless of age, begin your investment journey instead of buying your first home. Everyone's journey is different. Based on your circumstances, long term plan and income level, risk appetite, get your first investment property. Be comfortable with rent-vesting. Once you start thinking about investment, make a proper plan, stick to your plan, do enough research, due diligence and never look back in terms of buying property after property.

Most people buy one property and wait for three or four years, and they are unable to get back on track. Once you have the momentum, just keep that momentum going. Have a back plan A, B and C.

Don't give up. It is possible still in 2024. One of the investors that I am helping right now is only 27 years old. He is about to purchase his 4th property. They live in Sydney, but they didn't buy in Sydney. Their idea is to build a portfolio of 5 or 6 properties.

Ultimately, let's say if you buy 7 properties in five

years and let's say all of them are growing at 10%, you can sell two properties, get enough money, which would give you more than sufficient to purchase in Sydney after a few years.

Delayed gratification is everything in investment. And that's the most challenging part.

For people who might argue "I want to buy in Sydney, prices are already too high now. If I wait another 5 more years, it's going to be more expensive, and I may not be able to afford it. Let me buy my principal place of residence because I don't want to pay more later."

And let me be honest: No one wants to work a 9 to 5 job. Even, if you are a corporate lawyer or director or CEO, even if you are making $300,000k a year, people hate to go to work on Monday morning..

If you're going to buy that million-dollar property now, you're going to pay the mortgage for the next 30 years working on Mondays that you hate.

Instead of that, let's say if you delay buying in Sydney, the price will be higher. However, your position will be different, right?

If you buy five investment properties each for $400,000, you have a two million property portfolio. The two-million property portfolio will become a three-million portfolio in five years, right?

What did you do with your money?

You've already increased your wealth anyway. You might feel that you've missed the Sydney boat. But on the other side, you've created something for yourself.

Compare a 1-million-dollar house mortgage on one house to a few investment properties-which one would give you more sleepless nights?

You are getting five different rental incomes; five different rental streams and you have less risk.

Imagine you buy a million-dollar home and if you lose a job, what will happen?

You have to sell them anyway, because you will put all of your savings into a million-dollar home.

You would say, "Bharat, isn't that the same with having 5 investment properties? What if I lose my job, wouldn't I have to sell them?"

When you have five investment properties and if everything is easily managed through your tenants, you can claim through tax. Even if something happens, you get something in your pocket anyway. You don't have to be financially stressed.

I know it's hard to believe and hard to digest. There are lots of emotions. My wealth is my backup plan.

Another question that you might have: If my holding cost for each property is $600 a month and I have 5 properties, I have to spend $3,000 out of pocket. Isn't that too much?

My response would be: In reality, you are growing your 2-million-dollar property portfolio at 10% annual growth. That is $200,000 growth each year.

Let's say if you are losing $3,000 a month, right!

At the end of the year, it will be $36,000 dollars. You've made $164,000 in that year. **Spend money to make money.** Treat investment like a business. Extract $164,000 as equity and use that for your next investment. Initially use your money, and then you use the bank's money to make money. It's all about compound growth.

And you have rental income, so by increasing rent of $20 a week on five properties, it's $400 a week. Understand the system, understand leveraging, take the equity out, and then repeat the process until you generate enough for yourself.

This phase is called the acquisition period. You acquire properties one after another. Then the time comes, you can always do that consolidation.

This is like a game of understanding finance. Before you start investing yourself into property you need to understand finance and how it works.

If you're reading this book and realise "Hey Bharat, but I've already gotten my PPOR. I want to invest now. What should I do?"

Let's say if you don't have any borrowing capacity left over at all with one bank, go to another bank. And seek help from an investment-savvy broker. Just because one bank or broker says no, don't take that for an answer. Ask them why you don't have enough borrowing capacity. Ask them relevant questions. Ask them for solutions. For each obstacle, there is a solution. Seek that solution and take action. Sometimes, these solutions may not be the best thing you want to hear.

Again, zero emotions when it comes to property investing. Let the numbers speak to you. If it makes sense, then go ahead. Sometimes, it could be something out of your comfort zone. Growth happens out of your comfort zone.

Holding a property is a key. If you can't hold the properties, you can't see growth. Here, good debt plays an important role.

One observation that I noticed, especially among migrants moving to Australia, is that they are easily influenced by their peers, colleagues and family back in their home country. Because the first question they would be asked is, "oh, you're living in Australia for some time already, when are you going to buy your home?"

This would probably tempt you to make some mistakes of buying your overpriced principal place of residence because they fall into this peer pressure.

Think logically. Don't listen to advice from people who aren't savvy investors. I don't take any advice from anyone if they are not experts. There is always going to be pressure from everywhere. You may even go to your friend's housewarming function one day and the friend might nudge you to buy in the same suburb. Why would you want to slog like your friend who probably needs to work for the next 30 years to pay for this one house? Is that what you want?

Look, to be honest with you, yes, there is peer pressure. But it's up to you to take the pressure, or you can go to the right advisor to get the best advice. At the end of the day, your future is in your hands.

To build my 30-property portfolio, I educated myself. I didn't get trapped into friends or family pressure. And my next goal is to enter the commercial property market.

My second goal is to upgrade my home with bigger and better features.

I'm coming to the end of my book now, my friendly advice is: Buy your investment properties where you can get good equity to buy the subsequent ones. Because the first few properties are like a foundation, rinse and repeat the cycle.

If you make a mistake, you can't scale up, you can't grow, and you can't move on. Those first few properties are very important, whatever age you are buying, wherever you are buying, as long as you stick to those fundamentals then it will be very easy for anyone.

Buying the Right Property in the Right Order Is the Key to Building a Property Portfolio: Mr Patel's First 30 Properties Across Australia

Property No	Year of Purchase	Purchase Price
1	2010	$308,000
2	2012	$65000 - Granny Flat
3	2015	$422,000
4	2015	$85,000 - Granny flat
5	2018	$158,000
6	2018	$335,000
7	2016-2018	$860,000
8	2019	$50,000
9	2020	$65,000

10	2020	$65,000
11	2020	$491,750
12	2021	$60,000
13	2021	$107,000
14	2021	$110,000
15	2021	$96,250
16	2021	$290,000
17	2021	$210,000
18 and 19	2022	$208,000
20	2022	$342,500
21	2022	$260,000
22	2023	$250,000
23	2023	$260,000
24	2023	$154,000
25	2023	$350,000
26	2023	$450,000
27	2023	$390,000
28	2023	$430,000
29	2023	$630,000
30	2023	$490,000

Now that you've read my journey, what does it mean for you? This book is not just for me to share my journey. I want you to know that it is certainly something you can achieve too. You can be at any stage of your life right now. All you need is the right mindset, a long-term plan and confidence to get started.

1.What is the most important lesson you've learnt from this journey?

_____

_____

_____

2. What is the biggest challenge you think you'll face as a new investor??

_____

_____

_____

3. What's one thing you can do tomorrow to start your property investment journey?

_____

_____

_____

4. How can you save more money to invest in property?

_____

_____

_____

5. What's the best way to learn more about property investing?

_____

_____

_____

Chapter 7

Conclusion

I hope you enjoyed my genuine and honest story of building a property portfolio, which began in 2008 with no experience, a low income, but with a strong dream to achieve financial freedom within 10 years.

In property investment, success comes from self-awareness, a strong mindset, and taking action. Age is never a barrier. It's only a negative mindset that can hold you back.

Are you ready to change your mindset? If so, it's never too late. Australia is a land of amazing opportunities, attracting thousands of immigrants every year. As a result, there will always be a good time to build your own property portfolio.

My journey started in 2004 when I began university with a $36,000 debt. However, I made a firm decision to become debt-free and create a passive income within a decade.

By 2008, after obtaining my permanent residency, I committed myself to maintaining a strong mindset and never looked back. My journey is proof that confidence in yourself, combined with the right system and resources, can lead to success.

But it's not just my story but many of my clients have achieved incredible results as well. Let me share one inspiring example.

The Success Story of Ashok and Asha

Ashok and Asha, a couple in their late 30s with two children, aspired to achieve financial freedom through multiple property investments. After learning about my achievements, they sought my guidance. Their journey began in December 2022, and within a year, they built a portfolio of 12 investment properties.

Here are the first five properties they secured through our buyer's agency:

First Property
- **Location:** QLD
- **Purchase Price:** $425,000
- **Settlement:** January 2023
- **Projected Valuation (2025):** $565,000

"Bharat secured this solid brick house for us next to Toowoomba CBD," said Ashok.

Within three months, they secured four more properties in QLD through simultaneous contracts and settlements.

"It was a mammoth task to settle four properties at nearly the same time. It required a lot of preplanning, strategy, and teamwork," Ashok said.

Second Property
· **Location:** QLD
· **Purchase Price:** $467,000
· **Settlement:** February 2023
· **Projected Valuation (2025):** $634,000

We secured this property in the Rockhampton region, where vacancy rates are below 1% and stock levels are low. We helped Ashok and Asha acquire two high-value properties below market price with simultaneous settlements.

Third Property
· **Location:** Regional QLD
· **Purchase Price:** $355,000
· **Settlement:** March 2023

· **Projected Valuation (2025):** $500,000

Fourth Property
· **Location:** Regional QLD
· **Purchase Price:** $315,000
· **Settlement:** March 2023
· **Projected Valuation (2025):** $582,000

In under five months, they secured their final property—a fixer-upper in Townsville—where the bank valuation at the time of signing was $360,000.

Fifth Property
· **Location:** Regional QLD
· **Purchase Price:** $318,000
· **Settlement:** April 2023
· **Projected Valuation (2025):** $491,000

The Results

In less than two years, these five properties alone increased in value by $892,000. After this success, we helped Ashok and Asha acquire seven more properties in different states, diversifying their portfolio.

"We are grateful to Bharat for helping us build a massive property portfolio in just one year. Our story was even featured in The Courier Mail."

Client Testimonial: Ashok & Asha

❖❖❖❖❖ Highly Recommended

"It was a pleasure working with someone who truly understands property investment. Bharat and his team at Cashflow Properties identified our borrowing capacity and sourced multiple properties in a short period. From finding the properties to managing rentals, they provided a seamless, end-to-end service.

If you're considering investing in property, I highly recommend seeking Bharat's expert advice before making a purchase."

Where is Bharat Now?

In 2022, my wife and I decided to leave our corporate jobs to celebrate our success in acquiring 20 properties. During our two-month vacation, we realized that many people have the potential to build wealth through property investment but lack the right resources and time.

This realization led to the birth of **Cashflow Properties**—a buyer's agency I initially ran from my home office. In the first two months, we closed eight property deals for clients. As demand grew, we expanded our operations and built a dedicated team.

About Cashflow Properties

Today, Cashflow Properties is a leading buyer's agency specializing in finding affordable investment properties for investors.

Our Mission: Helping You Build Wealth Through Property

We believe property investment should be accessible to everyone, regardless of budget. Our expertise lies in identifying high-growth, affordable properties that provide strong returns without requiring a massive upfront investment.

Why Invest in Affordable Properties?

· **High Rental Yields** – Lower property prices often result in proportionally higher rental yields, boosting cash flow.

· **Sustainable Capital Growth** – Emerging areas can see substantial value appreciation as demand rises.

· **Risk Mitigation** – Spreading investments across multiple properties helps balance risk and strengthens your portfolio.

From property sourcing to purchase negotiations and settlement, our team handles the entire process, ensuring a stress-free investment experience.

Are You Ready to Build Your Property Portfolio?

I look forward to helping you secure your financial future through strategic property investments.

Thank you for reading my journey and learning how property investment can work for anyone with the right mindset and determination. Wishing you all the best in your investment journey!

If you would like to know more about property investing, visit *https://www.cashflowproperties.com.au/*, or grab your phone to call us at 1300 513 825.

The Checklist to Buy Your Investment Property

If you're thinking of investing in your first investment property, this checklist is going to be useful. I'm going to answer all your questions in one go.

1. I want to buy an investment property. Where should I start?

You need to understand your end goal. Your investment timeframe (10 years or 20 years) and the passive income you need to achieve.

2. How would I know my end goal?

Ask yourself if you need 70K or 80K or more for your annual expenses. For instance, when I started my investment journey my goal was to have a net rental income of 100k yearly before I reached the age of 40. And then I worked backwards to calculate the number of properties I needed.

3. Now I have my end goal, what's my next step?

Let's say your monthly income before tax is $8,000 and your goal is to have 100k passive income. Now you need to plan from point A to point B. What people do is to start looking for a property without a plan. That's the mistake many investors make without having a proper plan.

4. What does a proper plan look like? Who do I approach first?

Write down your risk appetite, your age, the time frame, your current income. Then you approach an investment-savvy broker. Not any kind of broker. Someone who has investment properties themself (if possible), or someone who has helped investors.

5. What does the broker plan for me?

They will assess your household income/other loans and inform you of your borrowing capacity. Let's say you can borrow up to 800K. You don't buy an 800K investment property first, because it will max out all you have. You can't borrow more or invest in more properties. If you can't buy more, you can't diversify your portfolio. Start with a property in the range of 300-400K first.

6. Ok, now I know my borrowing capacity. How much do I need to get started and what are the other costs involved?

If you are going to buy your first property at $350,000, including all the costs (conveyance fees, stamp duty, building and pest inspection fees), you need about $80,000.

7. How do I get my 2nd property and subsequent ones?

That system is called leveraging. Leveraging means you buy affordable property under market value. Buy a property where it is rising in value. After 3 to 6 months, you can refinance and take out equity to buy the next property. Let's say the property has grown in value by 40k in 6 months. You can take a portion of it. With your own savings and equity, you get your next 80k ready. That's how you build your portfolio gradually. It's purely a numbers game.

8. What if I don't have a 20% deposit? Can I go with 5% or 10%?

To begin with, a 20% deposit is always ideal because you can hold your property for a long time. Once I have two or three properties and then depending on what's my next goal, the ideal deposit would be 14 to 15% only.

A 5% deposit is a less-than-ideal starting point. With

such a low deposit, it will take longer to reach a more favourable 80% LVR, which is necessary for better loan terms and quicker equity growth.

9. What kind of research would help me choose the right property?

Understand the market level first. Then narrow down to the property level. You should buy in a market where it is going to boom in the next 5 to 7 years. Once you select the market, then you should narrow down your suburb selection.

Now, before you do the market research, remember the question you need to ask yourself, what is the motive of the property? Why am I buying this property? What can it make me for the next property?

News articles and websites might say Perth is a good area, or Queensland is a good area. But then you have to step back and do your numbers: If a suburb has already grown too much, do I invest there? Or do I look for another suburb?

In terms of the market research, instead of asking a silly question to someone who doesn't know about you and your circumstances, get yourself investor friends or seek professionals for help.

10. What websites can I get information from?

There are paid ones like DSR data and other free tools like SQM Research.

11. How do I choose the right suburb?

After your research, if you have listed 10 suburbs, further shortlist them according to: median price, days on market, proportion of renters, proportion of owners, kind of the people living in suburbs, any good schools, industries in that suburb, the ripple effect from that nearby suburb. If that suburb is too hot and everyone is buying, look at the next nearest suburb. Rental yield is another important factor.

12. How do I choose the right property?

When choosing a property, my ideal choice would be to avoid the shopping centre. Property ideally should be in mostly owner-occupied streets and fewer renters. I would look at the industry of that particular market and how professionals are living there and how my tenants will be. A brick home and avoid anything with structural issues. The layout of the land should be rectangular. Avoid corner homes.

13. How do I contact a sales agent?

I have a different approach for this. Don't contact the top agents. They don't have time for you. Go for the smaller property management companies and real estate companies. They're more approachable and you can negotiate better.

14. When do I put in the offer? What are the conditions I put in the offer?

Your offer and conditions like the finance clause and building and pest clause and electrical inspection clause. If the sellers want a longer settlement, I adjust accordingly. And always email your offer rather than over the phone. Once you email, follow up with the agent on the same day and ask them to send the contract. You need to show the sales agent that you're a serious buyer.

15. What if my offer is rejected?

Mostly, it is because of pricing. Ask the seller 'what would be the closing price deal?' They may not reveal all the details. You place another offer with 5k or10k more.

16. What happens after signing a contract? (building and pest/property manager inspection/

get insurance done/inform broker to get final loan approval)

After signing the contract, make sure you really check your names for any mistakes. Get help from the property manager for a property manager inspection, building & pest inspection and electrical inspection. Meanwhile, ask your broker to get the final loan approval letter ready.

17. What happens after a building and pest report and electrical and plumbing inspection report are received?

Read through the report and identify the major and minor concerns. Based on the major ones, you can negotiate with sellers to fix the issues or ask for a price reduction. Again, in a hot market, the sellers may not feel obliged to negotiate.

Look at the numbers again. If you know it is going to give back good returns in the next 6–12 months, would you let go of this property because of the maintenance issues? Let numbers give you the answer, not your emotions or ego.

18. How do you negotiate with the sales agent with the reports?

If it is a structural issue or an active termite issue, it is something major. If you have concerns, call the inspector and verify again. You must also understand this is not a brand-new building. Every property is going to come with maintenance issues.

Let's say the sellers are reducing it by $5,000 to do the bathroom renovation but you know, $5,000 may be too little for bathroom renovation. You can go back and ask for an $8,000 reduction. They may come back to a midpoint.

Negotiation is part of the game, and you must be mentally ready for it. Again, let numbers speak, and not your emotions.

19. When it goes unconditional, what do you do?

From an unconditional date, the first thing you need to do is hire a good property manager to manage your property. Before you find someone, you need to know their local reviews, their work, how they manage previous clients. Communicate clearly with your property manager: their fees, services, what is included, what is excluded, how many times they inspect the property, how many times they send you the inspection report throughout the year.

20. On the settlement date, what happens?

Before this, request your property manager to do a pre settlement check. Just ensure the house is in good condition and the fixtures and lighting are working.

On the settlement date, the conveyancer will arrange the settlement. They will send you the settlement statement. You confirm the settlement figures are correct, and they send you a congratulatory email on the day of the settlement. This indicates that your property manager can collect the keys and files related to the property from the previous managing agent.

21. How do you choose tenants from the PM's list?

Property managers always take care of the tenant selection but at the end you need to be aware of the quality of the tenant: IDs checked, verification of 100 points, employment status, previous lease record, if they pay rent on time, any criminal record, do they have pets.

22. When do you refinance next to get your next investment property?

After 3 to 6 months, get the ball rolling. You need to keep the momentum going. Accumulate as fast as you can. Get equity out from property 1 and your savings, go for the next property.

23. What happens if there is a maintenance issue?

Some tenants are good. Some are demanding. When you receive a maintenance email from your PM, see if it is an urgent one. If it requires immediate attention, better to solve it then. If it is a problem that can wait for another year or so, then just keep it on record, and you don't have to do anything. If you're spending about $500 on maintenance, you can claim it at the end of the financial year. Also, if your $500K property is growing at 10% a year, that is $50,000. You should be ready to spend $500 on something minor. Again, let numbers give you the answer.

24. Do I have to check in with the PM regularly?

Property managers should remind you of rent increases and other property-related expenses. But as an investor, you should also check in during quarterly inspection checks. When there is lease renewal, some property managers might just go, "market rate is $410." On your part, check the real estate website and verify the current asking rent. You can get your PM to request it for $430. In a hot market, tenants would like to secure a place.

Every rent increase is going to increase your cash flow and your borrowing capacity for the next purchase. But you can also be a kind landlord by doing what you can within your limits. I heard of landlords where they give 1 week of rent-free accommodation during the Christmas period. Some landlords present hampers, or New Year gifts for the current tenants. Again, it is your choice. Do good, be good.

People ask me, "What is my favourite property out of the 30?"

Property 15. Purchased at $96,250 at auction in Regional NSW. Spent $ 30K to renovate the property, and it was valued at $ 290K in 5 months.

Thank you for reading my journey and understanding how property investment can work for anyone who has the right mindset and determination. I wish you all the best in your investment journey. If you would like to know more about property investing, visit cashflowproperties. com.au or grab your phone to call us at 1300 513 825.

Making Moves!

A Snapshot of me in Action, Promoting my Business.

www.ingramcontent.com/pod-product-compliance
Lightning Source LLC
Chambersburg PA
CBHW040854210326
41597CB00029B/4837